PELL MELL

Civil War and Reconstruction in a Carolina Pocosin

K. Paul Johnson

Copyright 2021 K. Paul Johnson

This is a condensation of "Bertie Buffaloes," published in 2008 as Part Two of Pell Mellers: Race and Memory in a Carolina Pocosin.

Table of Contents

Introduction: Dismal Swamp Quakers on the Color Line 7

Chapter One: Despised Unionists 23

Chapter Two: Military Prisoners 35

Chapter Three: Planters' Sons 49

Chapter Four: Class War 61

Chapter Five: Johnson Reunions 73

Epilogue 81

Appendix 97

Endnotes 99

Sources Cited 103

6

INTRODUCTION

Dismal Swamp Quakers on the Color Line

John Henry Johnson [1874-1961] was one of eight brothers who left Bertie County around 1900 following disenfranchisement of black voters, which also made white Republicans and former Unionists like the Johnsons less welcome. Despite the prevalence of this theme in my father's family, the most dramatic stories about ostracism, exile and racial politics that I found in genealogical records involved my mother's Quaker ancestors along Little River in Pasquotank County, on the margin of the Great Dismal Swamp.

Some of the earliest Quaker settlers fled to North Carolina after being persecuted by local authorities in Massachusetts. After many generations in the Albemarle Sound region they became political outcasts there because of their opposition to slavery, and Quakerism became extinct in Pasquotank County after the Civil War. Several ancestors were disowned by the Friends meeting for a series of infractions; the most shameful incident unearthed in my years of genealogical research involved the disowning of my third great grandfather John Morgan. He lived in what is now Okisko along the upper reaches of Little River, which forms the border between Pasquotank and Perquimans counties.

Quakerism was the first organized religion in the Carolinas, arriving in the Albemarle region with the first English settlers in the 1660s. For a century Friends predominated in the region. Some Quakers arrived directly from England, but most came from Virginia and New England in the wake of persecution. The oldest Quaker colony in America was in southeastern Virginia and northeastern North Carolina, where the first monthly meeting, Perquimans, was established in 1680 and the second, Pasquotank, in 1698. The Albemarle Sound region had been home to Quakers since 1665, but visiting Irish missionary William Edmundson held the first organized Friends meeting in the spring of 1672 at the home of Henry Phillips, first Quaker colonist in North Carolina. My earliest North Carolina Quaker ancestor Francis Toms became a convert at that first meeting and held the next in his own home.

Settlement began along Perquimans River and by the end of the seventeenth century had spread to all the other streams draining the Great Dismal Swamp and flowing into the Albemarle Sound. A few months after Edmundson's visit, George Fox, founder of the Quaker movement he had led for more than twenty years, included the Perquimans River Friends on his missionary tour of the American colonies. The North Carolina Yearly Meeting was founded at home of Francis Toms in 1698.[1] Three monthly meetings had been established in Perquimans County in 1681, one at Christopher Nicholson's home, but the first three meeting houses were not constructed until 1704-1706.[2] Francis Toms was "a member of the Council, Deputy Collector of Customs, and Justice of the Peace" and his son-in-law Gabriel Newby was a member of the General Assembly.[3] Friends were prominent among colonial officials at the beginning of the 18th century, but were excluded from office by a 1710 requirement for all officeholders to swear oaths.[4] This occurred as Edward Hyde became governor. Under his predecessor, the Quaker governor John Archdale, Indians had been treated with respect as they were in Pennsylvania, but the year after Hyde became governor the Tuscarora War erupted with effects still felt throughout the region today. In late 1711 European settlements along the Neuse, Roanoke, and Trent rivers were attacked by the southern Tuscarora and allied tribes. By the end of the war in 1715 hundreds of colonists and thousands of Indians had been killed in the conflict.

The most memorable story of religious persecution of Quaker ancestors I found in family history involved the Nicholson family of Marblehead, Massachusetts. After Edmund Nicholson drowned in 1660, his wife Elizabeth and sons Christopher and Joseph were accused of killing their father and husband by means of witchcraft. In *New England Judged by the Spirit of the Lord*, this passage is addressed to the Magistrates of Boston:

> And to this let me add a cruel tragedy of a women of Marblehead near Salem and her two sons, Elizabeth Nicholson and Christopher and Joseph, whom you without ground charged with the death of Edmund Nicholson, her husband and their father, who was found dead in the sea; you having received information from some wicked spirits (like yourselves) that the people did shew love sometimes to the people of the Lord, whom you call cursed Quakers, your rage soon grew high against them, and unto your butcher's club at Boston you soon had them all three; and from prison you had them to the bar to try them from their lives; but notwithstanding all your cunning and subtile malice, to destroy the mother and her children at once, yet ye were not able; notwithstanding you fined her a great sum…and her two sons to stand under the gallows certain hours with ropes about their necks and to be whipped in your market place which was performed with many bloody lashes…and at Salem they were ordered to be whipped also…where it was so mercilessly done that one of the young men sunk down, or dyed away under the torture of his cruel

suffering, whose body they raised up again and life came to him.⁵

Christopher Nicholson, who had been born in England and brought to Marblehead as a child, married Hannah Redknap in 1662 and left for the Albemarle two years later. There he became a Quaker leader whose home was used for meetings during the missionary visits of George Fox and William Edmundson. He was arrested during the Culpepper Rebellion of 1677, in which the Albemarle colonists imprisoned the royal governor and replaced him with one of their own choosing. Two years later, he signed a petition in protest of abuse of Quakers by the colonial government. His first wife died in 1678, and two years later his marriage to Ann Atwood at the home of Francis Toms was the first event recorded in the minutes of the first monthly meeting in America.

Two of my Bertie County ancestors who fought in the Civil War were sons of planters, but none owned slaves. My only slaveholder ancestor who served in the Civil War was my mother's great grandfather William Twine White, who lived in Pasquotank County on the upper reaches of Little River. In 1860 his real estate was valued at $12,000, with $6309 in personal property. He owned eight slaves the same number his father Thomas White had owned when he died in 1839.

In the early nineteenth century many Quakers had left the state to avoid living under the slave system, as other abandoned Quakerism rather than free their slaves as required by their faith. The Civil War accelerated these processes, and the Quaker population of North Carolina declined by sixty percent between 1860 and 1868.⁶ My Methodist grandmother Eva Haskett was the descendant of many Albemarle families who had adopted the Quaker faith in the late seventeenth century and remained Friends into the early nineteenth. But political pressures from both Quaker authorities and North Carolina officials caused many Friends in northeastern part of the state to leave the region or convert to local Protestant churches in the decades before the Civil War. Wiliam White owned slaves and fought briefly for the Confederacy, yet his ancestors had been at the forefront of the manumission movement among local Quakers. William's great-grandfather Thomas White was summoned to the county court in 1783 on a charge of freeing his slaves illegally, and the same charge was made against another of his great-grandfathers, Benjamin Albertson, in 1788.[7]

William and his wife Axey, both children of Quaker parents, witnessed the collapse of Quakerism along the Little River in the early nineteenth century. Friends historian Stephen B. Weeks, a Pasquotank native, pinpoints 1811 as the year that "definite migration to the West began." By 1846 the Symon's Creek Monthly Meeting counted only fifty-five members and in 1854 both it and the Little River preparative meeting were "laid down."[8] In his study of North Carolina Quaker history, Hiram Hilty concludes that "discouragement over the question of slavery played an important role in this exodus from the Eastern counties."[9] Nevertheless, many who left remained in North Carolina, where they continued anti-slavery activism in the western Piedmont counties of Randolph, Yadkin, and Guilford. Quaker abolitionism extended into east Tennessee during the first third of the nineteenth century. Membership of the Quaker-led North Carolina Manumission Society declined sharply after 1831, in the wake of harsh new legislation inspired by the great slave insurrection led by Nat Turner in Southampton County, Virginia.[10]

Nat Turner's rebellion played a pivotal role in my

family history, as evident in monthly meeting minutes for several months following the event. Axey's father John Morgan was disowned in late 1831 by Symons Creek Monthly Meeting for "hiring a substitute [soldier], offering a reward for every negro he should kill, and for not attending meeting." The committee appointed to investigate the charge reported back in the minutes of November 19 that he "justified himself in his conduct." The committee recommended that he be disowned, and the minutes of the December meeting confirm that this was done.[11] The likely justification for compliance was that militia duty was a legal requirement of the state, and the only way to avoid it was to hire a substitute. But the Friends meeting could not accept such expediency and disowned John Morgan on the eve of his daughter's birth.

Nat Turner had been an itinerant evangelist for several years before he became leader of the most successful slave insurrection in North American history. In August 1831, a slave uprising inspired by Turner's visions had claimed sixty white victims in Southampton County, Virginia. At least twice as many blacks died in the resulting bloodbath, many of them innocent victims of white vigilantes. In North Carolina, the slave insurrection had evoked extreme violence among the whites near the Dismal Swamp, which John Morgan's farm adjoined. Turner's stated objective had been to flee to the Swamp where he would instigate a general insurrection with the support of the runaway slaves in the Great Dismal. Neither he nor any of his supporters made it out of Southampton County, but the free blacks and escaped slaves of the Albemarle region paid a huge price for Turner's fantasies. In *The Price of Liberty: African Americans and the Making of Liberia*, Claude Andrew Clegg III points out that "The Great Dismal allowed Pasquotank slaves to breach the confines of their thralldom in ways not available to most North Carolina bondspeople."[12] The presence of a significant number of runaways in the Swamp gave rise to exaggerated fears among the local whites in the wake of the Turner insurrection. Pasquotank had been a stronghold of the Quaker efforts to resettle freed slaves in Liberia; Clegg explains that "abolitionist sentiment among Pasquotank Quakers emerged from generations of slaveholding and a gradual reckoning with the iniquities of the practice."[13]

Fears of insurrection were widespread throughout the state after the Turner rebellion, when false rumors of a black army burning Wilmington and marching on Raleigh caused many slaves and free blacks to be rounded up and in some cases executed.[14] The *Edenton Gazette* noted on September 8 that "a large number of citizens from counties bordering on the Dismal Swamp, commenced yesterday to scout this great rendezvous for runaway slaves %c."[15] The panic was greatest in the Albemarle counties, and a vivid eyewitness account of the chaos in Edenton, the region's metropolis, is found in Harriet Jacobs's *Incidents in the Life of a Slave Girl*. In 1831 Jacobs was the slave of Dr. James Norcom and mother of two children fathered by neighboring white planter Samuel Tredwell Sawyer. She lived with her grandmother in Edenton where she observed the muster of militia:

> By sunrise, people were pouring in from every quarter within twenty miles of the town… Far as my eye could reach, it rested on a motley crowd of soldiers. Drums and fifes were discoursing martial music. The men were divided into companies of sixteen, each headed by a captain. Orders were given, and the wild scouts rushed in every direction, wherever a colored face was to be found… Those who never witnessed such scenes can hardly believe what I know was inflicted at this

time on innocent men, women, and children, against whom there was not the slightest ground for suspicion. Colored people and slaves who lived in remote parts of the town suffered in an especial manner...The dwellings of the colored people, unless they happened to be protected by some influential white person, who was right at hand, were robbed of clothing and every thing the marauders thought worth carrying away. All day long these unfeeling wretches went around, like a troop of demons, terrifying and tormenting the helpless. At night, they formed themselves into patrol bands, and went wherever they chose among the colored people, acting out their brutal will... No two people that had the slightest tinge of color in their faces dared to be seen talking together."[16]

That evening, Jacobs witnessed the increasingly drunken militia becoming a lynch mob that the townspeople came to fear as a danger to their own safety:

> The better class of the community exerted their influence to save the innocent, persecuted people; and in several instances they succeeded, by keeping them shut up in jail until the excitement abated. At last the white citizens found that their own property was not safe from the lawless rabble they had summoned to protect them. They rallied the drunken swarm, drove them back into the country, and set a guard over the town.[17]

Several weeks later, after Turner was captured, all the slaves and free blacks jailed in Edenton were released, but the small church they had built in the woods was demolished as protection against further subversion.[18] Turner's fame as an itinerant preacher contributed to white fears of blacks congregating in their own churches throughout the region. In 1835 Harriet Jacobs, fleeing harassment by Dr. Norcom, went into hiding in a tiny garret above her grandmother's cottage. There she remained for seven years until escaping to freedom in Philadelphia on a schooner in 1842. Her career as a writer, abolitionist, and advocate for freedmen continued for more than fifty years.

For five years in the 1980s I lived in Southampton County, a few miles down the road from Cross Keys intersection where Nat Turner's insurrection commenced in 1831. Although intrigued by the history of the insurrection, I had no idea at the time how had disastrously it impacted my mother's ancestors in North Carolina fifty miles across the Dismal Swamp…for the Quakers of Pasquotank County, a religious minority was driven to extinction by the racial politics of the color line.

Axey Morgan was born in February 1832, weeks after her father's expulsion from the Quaker community. John Morgan died in 1835, and his widow Margaret remarried within a year but died soon thereafter leaving Axey an orphan. Her prosperous uncle Seth Morgan, a Methodist minister and Elizabeth City storeowner, acted as guardian until the time of her marriage to William White. William and Axey were members of the Mount Herman Methodist Church where a plaque in their honor still hangs on the wall. Although Axey's parents died in their thirties, her grandmother Elizabeth Morgan was described as the oldest woman in Elizabeth City when she died in 1879, in the house owned by her son Seth which still stands in the historic district of the town. Axey's husband William enlisted as a Private in Company B (Stonewall Rifles) of the 17th Regiment of North Carolina Infantry (Confederate) on November 2, 1861, according to his receipt roll for the four month period ending March 1, 1862. His pay was eleven dollars per month. His muster roll dated May 30, 1862 gives his period of service as three years, and lists him as absent without leave. The roll for the period from May 1 to June 30 notes that he was absent from date of enlistment, meaning enlistment in the reorganized 17th Regiment after the original was disbanded in March 1862.[19]

Although his military career was very brief, William White was the subject of a vivid war memory that was carried down through the generations from my great grandmother Narcis White Haskett. Narcis, born in 1860, remembered that "when the Yankees came" they torched the family's home, and as it burned her family members were throwing their possessions out of the windows in order to salvage what they could from the conflagration. Historical records confirm this memory; the Whites' home was burned in a campaign of terror carried out in northeastern North Carolina by the still-controversial Union general Edward Wild. An old tape recording from 1953 was recently restored by a descendant of the William and Axey. In it, Narcis's younger sister recalled that when the White home was burned, William T. had fled into the Dismal Swamp and "there were five hundred blacks in the yard."[20] The "Yankee" army remembered by my great-grandmother was a black regiment led by a controversial white commander.

Edward Wild had returned to his home in Boston in December 1862 after battle wounds from the battle of outh Mountain caused the amputation of his left arm.[21] Governor John Andrews of Massachusetts conceived the idea of forming an all-black regiment, the 54th Massachusetts, and after several months in recuperation, Wild was asked by the governor to help in recruiting and training these troops.[22] In early 1863, Andrews had the idea of raising an additional 55th Massachusetts Regiment and then creating a new brigade. On April 13, Secretary of War Stanton authorized the raising of a brigade of four regiments of North Carolina blacks. On April 24th, Wild was appointed "Brigadier General of Volunteers," and by June the 55th Regiment was complete and mustered into service.[23] Black soldiers had already fought alongside whites in eastern North Carolina, when the town of Washington was under Confederate attack. Nonetheless, Wild encountered considerable resistance and hostility to his aims in the Union army. Recruiting began on May 15 in New Bern, where about 8500 black refugees were living in camps.[24] Another colony of fugitive slaves was established on Roanoke Island and in June 1863 Wild was ordered to carry out plans to build a new town there. The following month, his duties in North Carolina were interrupted by the call for the 55th to join the 54th in the vicinity of Charleston.[25] The First North Carolina Colored Volunteers (35th Regiment US Colored Troops), made up mostly of freed slaves, was organized in June 1863 and in August combined with the 55th. After the fall of Battery Wagner in Charleston Harbor, Wild and his troops were ordered back to New Bern in October. Before he was able to resume recruitment of black soldiers, he was then ordered to Fortress Monroe, Virginia, where he arrived November 1, to assume command of 37,480 "colored troops."[26]

The war had been fairly quiet during the latter half of 1863 in northeastern North Carolina, despite some raids by armed bands. That fall, General Benjamin Butler was assigned to be in charge of Federal forces in the region, and he soon ordered Wild and his brigade to raid the area. His goals were to liberate slaves and send them to the colony on Roanoke Island or to the north, enlist soldiers in his brigade, and "clear the area of guerrilla forces and partisan rangers."[27] The raid began on December 5 as Wild started a march from his Norfolk headquarters to Elizabeth City. Wild led 800 men via the Dismal Swamp Canal road, while a second column of comparable size went by way of Great Bridge and Northwest Landing. On December 11, Wild occupied Elizabeth City easily with only two men wounded and one captured by guerrillas.[28] The townsfolk were terrified by the presence of armed blacks in the streets, but the town suffered less damage from uniformed soldiers than from roving bands of white guerrillas. The troops destroyed several camps of guerrillas in the swamp, but were unable to destroy the largest camp near Hertford due to transportation problems.

The most dramatic event of that campaign involved Wild's army taking white hostages, and one of the victims was Phoebe Munden, the remarried widow of my third great grandfather John Thompson. John had died a year after his daughter Sarah's 1857 marriage to William Haskett. Thompsons, Hasketts, and Mundens along Little River had been Quakers from the seventeenth century into the nineteenth, although all had fallen away by the time of the Civil War. On February 10, 1864, Phoebe's second husband William Munden provided a deposition in which he recounted what befell his wife at the hands of Wild's troops:

> Affiant's family was at his home in that county about five miles distant from the town of Elizabeth City. On the afternoon of same day affiant's wife, Phoebe Munden, was arrested at her home and brought to Elizabeth City. She was then confined in a room over a store with some fifteen or twenty others, of whom all but herself and another lady, Mrs. Elizabeth Weeks, wife of Pender Weeks, were men. Both ladies were tied by their hands and feet

and detained three days, and were liberated only temporarily and to satisfy the calls of nature. When permitted to leave for this purpose they were accompanied by a negro guard, who stood over them with muskets, and they were compelled to do this in a public street. They were then carried off, their bonds untied, with the enemy's forces. The wrists of affiant's wife were bleeding from the stricture of the rope with which she was tied when she left. Mrs. Munden was taken from her three children, of which the oldest is about ten and the youngest four years of age, and no white person left with them. A young woman who lived in the family made her escape. A friend went there to take care of them at night. When carried off she was allowed to carry no change of clothes nor any night clothes. When confined in the room at Elizabeth City the ladies were compelled to sleep on the naked floor without bed or bedclothes or other covering, and without fire. About the third night Dr. W. G. Pool prevailed on the officer of the enemy to permit blankets to be carried in, and after some delay consent was obtained. Neither of these ladies have returned, but, so far as affiant knows or can hear, are kept still in confinement. While at Elizabeth City, when Mrs. Munden would complain of her treatment, she has been cursed and told she would be hung. The facts stated are detailed by witnesses who know them of highest respectability, and are implicitly credited by affiant. During this invasion the enemy under Brigadier-General Wild hung Daniel Bright, burnt affiant's house and all it contained, stables, crop, and nearly everything on the premises. They also burnt the house of William T. White, a commissary to Company E, before it was attached to the regiment and afterward.[29]

Wild claimed to have taken his hostages to protect the safety of his captured soldier Samuel Jordan. He threatened to hang both women if Jordan were hanged by the rebels.[30] On December 17, Wild organized a court to try twenty suspected guerrillas. Nine were acquitted, but eight were convicted and sent to Norfolk. One, Daniel Bright, was sentenced to death by hanging, and executed the following day, with Mrs. Munden and Mrs. Weeks forced to watch.[31] The raid ended on the 21st and the troops returned to Norfolk and Portsmouth, leaving a small detachment that went to Knotts Island and captured another female hostage.[32] Letters immediately began to reach General Butler objecting to Wild's behavior in North Carolina as "acts of barbarity."[33] Private citizens initiated the complaints but soon Confederate officials were trying to get the hostages released, with Governor Vance threatening retaliation on Union troops for any harm that befell the hostages.[34] Complaints about wanton destruction of property by Wild's troops came both from Union and Confederate sympathizers.

Abraham Lincoln became involved in Wild's hostage-taking in mid-January, confronting General Butler and ordering him to rescind an order Wild had given for the execution of his hostages. Butler then ordered the release of the two women, the Knott's Island hostage having been already freed. The raid became increasingly controversial on both sides of the war, with a Confederate congressional investigation and strong criticism in a national newspaper, the *New York World*.[35] Finally, in April 1864, Wild was demoted to a lesser position. In July he was court-martialed and found guilty of disobeying an officer, but on appeal the verdict was overturned.[36]

The panic of 1831 was inspired by a mythical black army in the Great Dismal Swamp that existed only in the visions of Nat Turner. Three decades later, a real black army led by General Wild marched south through the Swamp to conquer the county where Quakerism had become a memory. Friends in the Albemarle country engaged in moral reflection about slavery from their seventeenth century origins, but found their manumission efforts thwarted in the eighteenth. In the nineteenth century, they advanced their anti-slavery cause through African colonization schemes while emigrating to Piedmont counties and Midwestern states in large numbers. The political aftermath of the Nat Turner insurrection left the remnant Pasquotank Quakers in an impossible position. John Morgan's ethical dilemma following the 1831 muster of militia symbolized the predicament of all Albemarle Friends. Conflicting demands of church and state led to continued emigration and ultimately the laying down of their meeting in 1854. First founded in 1682, the Little River meeting in various forms survived 172 years before succumbing to the polarized atmosphere of the approaching Civil War.[37]

Josiah Dunlow, 1840-1906

Chapter 1

Despised Unionists

Aunt Ethel was just six years old when her grandfather Josiah Dunlow died in 1906. In 1977 I interviewed her as part of a class assignment for a genealogy course in library school. On spring break, we were to find the oldest living members of each parent's family and ask them a series of questions, the first being "what are your memories of your grandparents?" Ethel called her grandfather Joseph rather than Josiah, and I later found other records using the same name late in his life. Her memories of him centered on one vivid incident that she enthusiastically retold. Several of Josiah's grandchildren lived in the vicinity, and a group of them was playing in the attic of his house. Ethel remembered a trunk in the attic that the children were expressly forbidden to open. Not surprisingly, they became so curious about its contents that they disobeyed the adults and opened it. The only thing inside was a blue uniform, Ethel reported with a grave expression, adding that when Josiah died a tombstone came from Washington D.C. and his family received a pension for his military service. That clue led me to military records, which confirmed that Josiah served in Company C of the First North Carolina Infantry (Federal) from 1862 through 1865. The only information readily available at the time about this regiment was that its members, called Buffaloes, were hated by local citizens for their criminal behavior. For more than a century after the war's end, there were no books offering sympathetic or even objective portrayals of Unionists in eastern North Carolina. But in recent years their story has emerged in several studies, two of which focus on Bertie County. 1300 men from eastern North Carolina served in the Union army, for reasons that are subject to several interpretations. In a brief regimental history, Donald E. Collins concludes that the first men to enlist in the First and Second North Carolina regiments were motivated by class conflict. A *New York Tribune* correspondent described them as having "bitter and malignant feelings toward their disloyal neighbors and hated slavery and slaveholders whom they believed responsible for their condition."[1] The poverty of small farmers in the region was so hopeless that they looked to a Union victory as deliverance from oppressors. As the war progressed, Confederate deserters swelled the ranks of North Carolina Union regiments. The army provided some financial security when it was becoming increasingly rare. Union enlistees were promised that they would not have to serve outside North Carolina, at a time when Confederate Carolinians were dying in tens of thousands outside the state. The Buffaloes served always under the protection of Northern troops, and rarely saw active combat.

    The Carolina coast was one of the first areas of Union victory in the Civil War. In August 1861 Hatteras was occupied by Union troops, and by the end of the year the entire coast north of New Bern was in the hands of Federals. The population of the Outer Banks strongly welcomed the Union presence, but loyalties were divided in the country along the Sounds. The First North Carolina Regiment originated in April 1862 in Washington, North Carolina after a Union force landed in the town. Enlistment posters appeared on May 1, addressed to "the people of Eastern North Carolina."[3] Company C, recruited almost entirely in the area of the Pell Mell Pocosin, included two of my direct ancestors and several of their kinsmen. Marcus Johnson enlisted at age thirty-one on July16, 1862, but deserted on January 14, 1863 and then was captured after eighteen months in hiding on July 14, 1864.

Courtmartialed for desertion in September 1864, he was sentenced to six months of hard labor, but released before the end of February 1865. Josiah Dundelow enlisted on August 7, 1862, at age twenty-two. The Company Descriptive Book records his height as 5 feet 10-3/4 inches, his complex- ion as dark, hair as black, eyes gray.[4] His war records show that he was absent for three months from September through November, for which he was "tried by Colonel Josiah Picket and pay stopped from enlistment to May 1863."[5] Hardy Johnson, Jr, twenty-three, Josiah's first cousin, enlisted on the same day. (Hardy's mother, Temperance Butler Johnson, was the older sister of Josiah's mother Susanah.) William H. Butler, first cousin of both Josiah and Hardy, enlisted in Company C at Plymouth on November 24, 1862, after deserting from Confederate Company B, Twelfth Battalion North Carolina Infantry.

The most significant engagement of Company C occurred in Plymouth in December 1862. On the morning of the tenth, Confederate artillery, cavalry and infantry attacked the Union garrison town and burned many buildings including the company's headquarters.[6] In March 1863, Company C was pulled out of Plymouth following a siege by Confederate troops that had lasted most of the month. They were reassigned to Washington and arrived there by late April.[7]

In his study *Bertie in Blue*, Gerald Thomas provides a context in which to understand the experience of the Unionists of the county. In 1979, Thomas was astounded to discover that one of his great grandfathers had fought for the Union, never having heard before of any Union presence in Bertie County. He devoted many years to documenting the Civil War history of the county, resulting eventually in two books that make the path much smoother for subsequent genealogical researchers, the second focusing entirely on the Unionists. Bertie provided 214 white citizens to the Federal forces as well as 349 former slaves. Eight whites and forty-nine blacks from Bertie joined the Union Navy from Bertie. 62 of the 222 Bertie whites in the Federal army had also served in the Confederacy.[8] Bertie Union soldiers saw less combat than their Confederate counterparts, but suffered a higher casualty rate. This is due to the Battle of Plymouth casualties which comprised fifty-four of the 105 Bertie Unionists present at the battle. Six were killed in action, with thirteen missing in action and thirty-five captured.[9] "Buffaloes" as an epithet for the North Carolina Union troops was synonymous with "thieves, deserters, and out- laws."[10] According to William H. Trotter, "The Unionists... formed a loosely knit network of outposts inside the no- man's-land north of Plymouth. Whether they were regulars, deserters, or common bandits, all of these men became known to the fearful and unprotected civilians as 'Buffaloes'."[11] Jonathan Mizell, Littleton Johnson, and Calvin Hoggard, all from the Pell Mell Pocosin area, were the commanders of Buffalo companies comprised of Bertie County men. Between mid-June 1862 and the end of the year, thirty-five Bertie men joined Company C of the First Regiment. Although Mizell's leadership produced excellent discipline in the company, the "Buffaloes" were regarded with some disdain by their northern colleagues. One Pennsylvanian described them as having "dark hair, sallow complexions, high cheek bones, long visages, a treacherous looking eye, a shuffling sort of a walk & almost any other ugly look that you can think of."[12] Other descriptions found in correspondence are "riff-raff," "ragged and rough looking," and "the strangest people in the world."[13]

Company C's first encounter with the enemy occurred on August 30, 1862 in a skirmish on the road west of Plymouth; there were no Union casualties but three Confederate men were killed and one captured.[14] Company C served under Captain William W. Hammell of Company F of the Ninth Regiment New York Infantry, until November when his company was replaced by Company I of the Third Regiment Massachusetts Infantry.[15] When the Confederate attack burned most of Plymouth in December, regimental commander Captain Barnabas Ewer abandoned his men and took refuge on the gunboat *Southfield*. Mizell's company performed well and he reported that "our little North Carolina volunteers behaved most nobly."[16] By this time Plymouth had becomea refuge for Unionist civilians black and white; in one week of November 1862, 420 took the oath of allegiance to the United States.[17] Mizell's full report to his commanding officer, Colonel Potter, explains the impact of the December attack:

> SIR: I resume my seat for the purpose of informing you of the attack the rebels made upon our little village, and I should judge from all the information I can gather and from what I saw they numbered some 450 strong—300 infantry, 3 pieces of artillery, and 70 cavalry. About 4.30 o'clock they drove our pickets in with a volley from their infantry, and in fifteen minutes our company was in line, and as the odds were too great for our little force I deemed it most prudent to fall back to the rear of the custom-house, and before we could all get in the building they had planted their pieces of artillery on the wharf and had fired some three rounds at the Southfield, and the third fire disabled her boiler. After they found she was disabled and dropped down the river they moved their field pieces on the corner opposite headquarters, but not without the loss of some men. They commenced to shell the

custom-house, and as they passed down the street in small groups our men would let the lead fly at them to best advantage, and I do assure you our little North Carolina volunteers behaved most nobly. They were calm and collected, much more so than I expected. Sergeant Clift was informed that the rebels lost 15 killed and 30 wounded, some mortally and some slightly, and the information he got yesterday corroborates the other statements we received. I heard they had four wagon loads of killed and wounded. Our men never received a scratch. The North Carolina cavalry lost 3 men prisoners and 1 wounded. Company I, of Massachusetts, lost 14 prisoners, 1 wounded, and 1 missing. One man on the Southfield lost a leg. We sustained considerable loss from fire. The best and most of the principal part of the town are burned up. The families of our men are left without a change of clothing, and they are in a distressed condition. Besides, we have lost all our books, pay, and muster rolls, and a quantity of clothing belonging to the men; some ammunition. They captured nothing from the Government, but pillaged private dwellings, &c. I believe I have given all the particulars that I can think of at present.

I must speak of something else in your last communication. You wrote to send the names of the twelve men that are to be transferred to the cavalry company, and inclosed you will find them on a piece of paper, and when you write to me I would be glad if you will send me the original muster-roll, so we can get the time of enlistment of them, as all of ours were destroyed by fire in Sergeant Clift's house, with all of his property. Also please send mea morning report book; monthly and weekly re- ports also. I should be glad to have a descriptive and company

clothing book; and by complying you will greatly oblige.
Your respectfully, &c.,
J. T. Mizell
First Lieut., Comdg. Company C., First N.C. Infantry
Col. E. E. Potter

P.S.—Dear Sir: We have not yet received our equipments that were left at Roanoke Island, and as soon as I can make it convenient I shall dispatch Sergeant Clift for them. Please answer soon.[18]

When Mizell resigned his commission on November 24, 1863, he was replaced by Lt. Albert Edwards of Trenton, New Jersey. The Second North Carolina Union Regiment was authorized in February 1863 but not organized until the end of the year. By then forty-nine Bertie men had joined company B, and another forty-one enlisted in company E, both assigned to garrison duty in Plymouth. Many soldiers were joined there by family members.[19] Jonathan Williford, who joined Company B at age 40 on January 1, 1864, is my only direct ancestor who served in the Second Regiment, but two collateral ancestors fought by his side. Most notable, and notorious, is Marcus's uncle Littleton Johnson, who was the first captain of Company B. He had previously deserted from Company G of the Thirty-Second Regiment North Carolina Troops of the Confederate army, as had Marcus from Company D of the same regiment.[20] Both had served only a few months in gray before deserting. Littleton's career as an officer in the Federal Army was also short-lived, as he was appointed Captain on February 2, 1864 but arrested on June 12 in Beaufort for "open and gross violation of discipline and endeavoring to incite mutiny among the men in camp."[21] This led to a discharge without trial on August 13.

Marcus's younger brother Haywood Johnson enlisted in Company B on October 25, 1863. Six weeks later, Josiah's thirty-eight-year-old uncle John Dundelow enlisted on December 1. Two other collateral ancestors were members of the company, but like John Dundelow neither survived the war. Eighteen-year-old John A. Cobb, younger brother of Marcus's future second wife Rutha, enlisted on December 14, 1863. Lorenzo White, who enlisted at age thirty-seven in New Bern nine days later on December 23, was brother of William White whose daughter Nancy became the wife of Josiah Dunlow.[22] The 1860 census shows Lorenzo and his wife Martha living on a farm adjacent to Elmore Dunlow's.

In January 1864, Companies B and E of the Second Infantry participated in raids of Confederate stores in Bertie County. In February, twenty-two Confederate deserters who had joined company F of the Federal Second regiment in New Bern were captured and hanged in Kinston after a skirmish, causing all Buffaloes to feel threatened by such reprisals.[23] When Captain Charles Foster ordered all companies of the First and Second to Beaufort for training, Calvin Hoggard protested and Foster relented, allowing Hoggard's and Johnson's units to remain at Plymouth.[24] The following month Foster, who had been controversial from the beginning of his service on the Outer Banks, was relieved of command for incompetence. His successor, Captain Walter S. Poor of the First Regiment New York Mounted Rifles, reported that Johnson's and Hoggard's companies of the Second North Carolina Union Volunteers were poorly trained and of little use to the army.[25] Poor reiterated Foster's original request for transfer of the companies to Beaufort "for discipline and instruction" but before it could be acted on Plymouth was under Confederate attack.

Although the town was protected by 2800 soldiers, four naval gunboats, and a system of defensive earthworks and forts, it fell to a Confederate assault by a force of 7000 men, accompanied by the ironclad *Albemarle* which had been constructed upstream on the Roanoke.[26] The assault began on April 17, 1864, and by evening of the 19th the downfall of Plymouth was inevitable. That night many Buffaloes escaped in canoes across the Roanoke, and on the morning of the 20th General Wessells formally surrendered.[27] Once the surrender of Plymouth became inevitable, Hoggard and Johnson ordered their men to escape as best they could. A Pennsylvanian wrote that they "made for the adjoining swamps, for they well knew their fate if they fell into the hands of their enemies."[28]

Many hiked northwards, through water up to three feet deep across the low grounds towards home, while others slipped through the lines and escaped in different directions. Some who could not flee donned uniforms of fallen northern troops and adopted their identities to avoid execution. Haywood Johnson was missing in action for several days after the battle, but was picked up by the Federal gunboat *Miami* on the shore of Albemarle Sound and returned to his regiment. John Dundelow was captured and taken to Andersonville prison where he died August 25, 1864 of scurvy. Of the twenty other Bertie County men imprisoned there, only one, Yancey Evans, came home alive. Jonathan Williford escaped from Plymouth and was missing in action until he returned to his unit in May. John A. Cobb was captured in battle and his fate remains unknown. Lorenzo White was among the Bertie men killed in action at Plymouth.[29] In that single battle, almost every Pell Meller family suffered a loss. Those Buffaloes whose identities were known by their enemies were subjected to "all the concentrated rage of the rebels" after captured Union soldiers were paraded before Confederate soldiers and former deserters were picked out.[30] Of 105 Bertie County men in the battle, six were killed, thirty-five were captured and the same number escaped and returned to duty; the remainder were missing in action.[31]

Company C in Washington became "intensely demoralized" on news of Plymouth's fall, and before evacuating Washington they plundered and ransacked the town, rampaging through homes and businesses, carrying away what they could and destroying the rest, before evacuating to New Bern on April 30. After the Battle of Plymouth, any black soldier caught in a blue uniform was killed.[33] Plymouth and Washington were rare examples of Confederates regaining territory that had been in Union hands.[34]

According to Fort Macon historian Paul Branch, even before the Battle of Plymouth, captures and executions of North Carolina Union soldiers created fears "so overpowering that the reliability and effectiveness of the two regiments as front-line troops began to diminish rapidly" and they became "a liability for the Union Army."[35] After the fall of Plymouth and evacuation of Washington, the First North Carolina Regiment was withdrawn to New Bern, accompanied by 300 women and children.[36]

A remnant of the Second was garrisoned in Morehead City, but after Plymouth fell they were "utterly demoralized and will not fight" according to Col. Edward H. Ripley's report to the District Commander.[37] Ripley proposed relocated them "out of harm's way" in Fort Macon, with the families in Beaufort.[38] For most of the last year of the war, four or five companies of the First Regiment were permanently stationed at Fort Macon for garrison duty, with the rest of both North Carolina Union regiments in the vicinity.[39] Branch concludes that "Despite the passage of 130 years, the North Carolina Buffaloes still elicit the strongest emotions of contempt and disdain for many North Carolinians."[40]

The Second Regiment remained at Beaufort from Spring 1864 through February 1865, when it was consolidated with the First. The First was mustered out on June 27, 1865, including 107 men from Bertie.[41]

Marcus Ryan Johnson, 1831-1916

Chapter 2
Military Prisoners

Each year the commemoration of the Battle of Plymouth includes the participation of descendants of the "Plymouth Pilgrims" who were captured and sent to Andersonville Prison. According to Civil War prison historian Ronnie Speer, Andersonville Prison was, "from day one, one of the most wretched places of confinement that words could describe."[1] Intended to hold eight to ten thousand prisoners, the camp was comprised of sixteen and a half acres enclosed by a stockade fence with only two trees left standing. Within a few weeks of the opening of a new portion of ten more acres, the prison population increased to 29,000.[2] By August, the population had reached its peak of nearly 33,000, and poor diet and sanitation caused many deaths from "scurvy, diarrhea, dysentery, typhoid, small-pox, and hospital gangrene."[3] Murder was as serious a threat to the prisoners as disease, and occurred daily. Guards and "raider groups" among prisoners were equally likely to commit murder, the most notorious of these raider groups being led by William "Mosby" Collins. By September the majority of prisoners were transferred out of Andersonville because Union forces had recently moved into the area.[4] Lonnie Speer's *Portals to Hell: Military Prisons in the Civil War* provides the most thorough account of the experience of more than 410,000 prisoners held in more than 150 compounds. 30,218 died in Confederate prisons, over 15% of the prisoners, and 25,796 died in Federal prisons, accounting for more than 12%. By comparison the percentage of deaths suffered by those who were never captured was 5%. Although many of the prisons were no more than concentration camps (Andersonville being the worst) Speer argues that neither government intentionally created conditions of pestilence and starvation in its prisons. He argues instead that the major factor was a total lack of preparation for war by both sides, neither of which envisioned the need for prisons holding hundreds of thousands of captives.[5]

    The descriptive book for Company C records Marcus Johnson as having red hair, blue eyes, a light complexion, and a height of 5 feet 11inches. He enlisted in Plymouth on July 17, 1862, for a term of three years. On my first visit to the Roanoke River museum in Plymouth, Harry L Thompson, its curator, devoted the better part of an hour to sharing stories of local history, showing me Johnson documents, and encouraging my investigations. Harry had many documents related to the Johnsons especially Marcus. The museum is a crucial resource for anyone whose ancestors were involved in the Battle of Plymouth. On the anniversary of the April 1864 battle each year there is a commemoration with a torchlight procession, reenactments in the streets of the town, and an elaborate encampment. Harry told me a family story of how Marcus supposedly became a Union soldier, which later proved doubtful in light of historical evidence. But the story is worth repeating for its oral history resonance, if not for its historical validity. The Confederates had begun conscription and a party was riding around the countryside summoning men to Windsor to enlist. Marcus was out plowing a field when they showed up, and came over when beckoned. He asked them what the pay was and they told him twelve dollars a month. He then asked "in what?" and they told him the pay was in Confederate scrip. Then Marcus sought out and found a recruiter for the Union army and asked the same questions; the answers were thirteen dollars a month, in gold. So he took a boat down the Cashie from Windsor to Plymouth that night and signed up with the Federals. When Marcus came home from the war with $500 in gold he used it to buy 700 acres north of

Windsor, where he raised a large family. I learned from Harry that my great grandmother Rutha had been Marcus's second wife, and that this was a second marriage for her too; also that her maiden name was Cobb, not Bird which was that of her first husband.

The implication of Harry's story was that Marcus was not strongly motivated by patriotism or principle, which his behavior as a soldier tends to confirm. Quarterly muster rolls show him present until the first quarter of 1863, but he deserted on January 14. His name next appears in a "descriptive list of deserters" dated Fort Macon, November 1, 1864, according to which he had deserted from Plymouth and was "captured" July 11, 1864. He appears to have turned himself in, as an additional report says that he "joined from desertion" at Fort Macon. A note from the Provost Marshal's Office in Morehead City, dated July 28, 1864, says that Marcus had been received at Fort Macon, "to be forwarded to New Bern." In the summer of 1864 he was listed as serving a sentence of General Court Martial at Fort Totten. The muster roll for August 31, 1864 to April 30, 1865, includes remarks on Marcus stating that six months pay had been stopped by "Genl Order #15 Hal. Mil. Dist of NC Sept 22 64." He was not listed as present again until 1865; the muster out roll dated June 27, 1865 specifies that his pay was stopped and adds a notation that he was tried and found guilty of desertion and sentenced to six months of hard labor and forfeit of all pay during the confinement.[6]

Fort Macon is the greatest fortification of the North Carolina coast, a "concentric series of sunken, irregular pentagons" with at the center an "open yard, or parade, enclosed by a labyrinth of rooms with a raised terreplein, which is encircled in turn by a moat and gently sloping outer embankment, called the glacis."[7]. It was designed in 1821 by French émigré Simon Bernard who had been Napoleon's military engineer, and constructed between

1826 and 1834. The site is now the most popular state park in North Carolina, although the adjacent beach probably accounts for the popularity more than the museum at the fort. The fort has been meticulously restored in recent years, with exhibitions depicting life there throughout the history of the site. One exhibit featured a Federal deserter wearing a blue uniform marked P for prisoner, which Marcus Johnson would have been obliged to wear during his confinement. It is never mentioned in any of Marcus Johnson's Union military papers that he had originally enlisted in the Confederate army, but deserted after only a few weeks. He lasted sixth months in the First Infantry before again deserting. In a recent study of Confederate deserters, Mark Weitz points out that North Carolina was stigmatized as having more deserters than any other state in the Confederacy, but also had the highest casualties and the largest number of troops in combat.[8] The most notorious Johnson deserter was Littleton, who enlisted in Company G of the Confederate North Carolina Thirty-Second Regiment on April 1, 1862 as a substitute, and was mustered in as a private at age thirty-eight. On November 1, 1862 he was promoted to Corporal, but on April 2, 1863 he was reduced to ranks, after which he deserted on May 12, 1863.[9] Among many causes for the high rate of desertion in the Confederate Army, the first was that soldiers' loyalties were primarily to local communities rather than to their states, and certainly more than to a Confederacy that had only existed for two months before the war. Secession had been fraught with controversy in three of the seven Deep South states, which were the first to secede, and in all of the Upper South states, which seceded after the Confederacy was first established.[10] Deserting to the Union army was considered far more shameful than mere desertion, an act of dishonor that "might follow a soldier into civilian life upon his return."[11] The common saying in the South that it was a rich man's war but a poor man's fight was accurate; the planter class included three percent of the Southern population but contributed far less than its fair share to the army. The soldiers were overwhelmingly drawn from the yeomen farmer class, whose families needed their labor at home.[12] As the war dragged on, men were motivated to desert because "home not only afforded certain comforts but also stood on the verge of ruin."[13] Saving home from ruin could risk permanent dishonor after the war, a theme explored in the novel *Hearthstones* by Bernice Kelly Harris. It describes the fate of the Day sisters, who were shunned by the community for decades as a result of their father's desertion from the Confederate army.

The lawless behavior of Confederate deserters so terrorized civilians in eastern North Carolina that it created public support for the Union, as a matter of survival.[14] By 1864, Plymouth was host to a large contingent of Confederate deserters as well as its Union garrison. Deserters used the town as a base from which to attack Bertie County plantations along the Roanoke and Chowan Rivers. Bertie County was unusual in that deserters carried out their raids on wealthy plantations and not just modest farms which was more typical across the state. Deserters added another element to a volatile situation in northeastern North Carolina. Local political rivalries between poor Unionists and rich pro-Confederate planters had led to guerrilla-style raids. Weitz points out that bands of deserters "confused the situation by preying on both sides with impunity, blurring any clear lines of demarcation and raising the level of anxiety."[15]

Marcus's unimpressive military career did not prevent him from receiving veteran's benefits. Writing to the Pension Office on March 1, 1884, Marcus applied for partial disability, claiming never to have recovered from the yellow fever and pneumonia for which he was treated in 1865 in the Morehead City hospital. Josiah Dunlow was one of his witnesses. Eleven months later, in February 1885, a letter from the Pension Office confirmed that Marcus had been hospitalized for these diseases in April 1865 and discharged in New Bern in June. On June 17, 1885, the Surgeon General's office gave the dates of his hospitalization as April 1 to June 27, 1865. No disability was approved before November 1890, when Marcus added the report that he was partially disabled by lung disease. On June 24, 1891, the medical examiner gave him a rating of 8/18 for lingering symptoms of yellow fever, but none for lung disease or hip injury. Yet when he finally got his Surgeon's certification of pension on August 28, 1891, the cited causes were eye disease and senility. On July 9, 1892, Marcus applied for additional pension funds on account of lung disease, pain in his right side and back, nervousness, piles, and old age. After he was examined for these complaints, it was reported on June 19, 1895 that no lung disease was found, nor evidence of back and side pain, and nervousness and old age were not serious problems. On February 12, 1896, Dr. Dunstan described his physical appearance as healthy and well nourished, with hard muscles and horny hands. In an 1898 report, Marcus stated that his first wife Mary died before the Civil War, Rutha died "about 9 years" earlier, and he married Roxana "about 4 years" ago. It lists eleven living children and does not mention either of the two borne by his first wife Mary.

On February 2, 1901, Marcus applied for a pension increase, claiming to be two thirds disabled. Six months later his pension was increased to eight dollars per month due to the loss of vision in one eye. Marcus personally testified under oath before a Justice of the Peace on March 15, 1902 that he "never rendered any service in the army or navy of the so called Confederate states during the war of the late rebellion prior to my enlistment into Company C, 1 NC Vol." This was perjury because he had deserted from the Thirty-Second Confederate Infantry before joining the Federal army, although whether he "rendered any service" during his brief time as a rebel is debatable.

On July 16, 1902, Marcus claimed total disability. Josiah Dunlow was witness to his debilitated condition. In response, his pension was increased to ten dollars per month on February 18, 1903, with bronchitis, rheumatism, and senile debility added to causes of invalidism. On April 27, 1904, his pension was in- creased again, to twelve dollars per month, on the basis of total disability; on March 20, 1907, increased again to twenty dollars, and on July 2, 1912, increased for the last time, to $22.50 per month. Marcus's death certificate states that hedied January 26, 1916 and was buried the next day, naming old age and "nephrite" as the causes of death. On May 27, 1916, Roxana was authorized as his widow, and on September 18, 1916, a pension approved for her. She was dropped from the pension rolls the month after her death on April 13, 1924. She resided at the time of her death with her stepson Ulysses Johnson and his family a Hull Street in South Norfolk.

Marcus's younger brother Thomas Haywood Johnson also was a Buffalo, but unlike Marcus and their uncle Littleton he had never served in the Confederate army. When he enlisted on October 23, 1863, he was thirty years old, 5'7 inches, with a fair complexion, grey eyes, and light hair. He first enrolled in Company C of the Second North Carolina Infantry, which was later consolidated into Company D of the First. He was briefly missing in action after the Battle of Plymouth but found on the shore of Albemarle Sound and rescued by the naval gunboat Miami on April 22, 1864. Haywood was mustered out with the rest of his regiment on June 27, 1865 in New Bern. His first disability request was made on June 27, 1890, based on claims of failing eyesight and bladder disease, but rejected on January 30, 1894. Later that year he applied again, claiming rheumatism and kidney disease as disabling conditions, and was finally approved June 6, 1896. Another claim was submitted May 14, 1897 for the same conditions, and in December 1898, Haywood asked for an increase from six dollars per month. On January 3, 1899, he added lung disease and asked again for an increase; this was rejected on May 4, 1900, but on August 16, 1902, his pension was increased to eight dollars per month. Haywood immediately applied for another increase to ten dollars, which was granted January 12, 1904, adding senility and heart disease to the list of debilities. Further increases occurred on May 3, 1904 (twelve dollars), March 15, 1907 (fifteen), and March 5,1909 (twenty dollars, because past age 75.). Among those providing affidavits for him was J.R. Williford, 32 in 1894. Haywood Johnson died on January 27, 1911, and his pension was ordered dropped on Feb. 9.

When Jonathan Williford enlisted for a term of three years on January 1, 1864, he was a forty-year-old farmer, six feet tall with brown hair and blue eyes. The recruiting officer was Captain Littleton Johnson, his brother-in-law. Jonathan was promised a bounty of three hundred dollars, and awarded the first installment of sixty dollars at the end of April. At this point he was missing in action for a few days following the Battle of Plymouth, just four months after enlisting. After returning to duty in May he was assigned to service in New Bern (Carolina City), where was at work building quarters by October. By the end of the year he had received the remaining installments. At the beginning of 1865 he was transferred to the First North Carolina Volunteers, Company E, and assigned to Beaufort. There is some confusion in his pension records about whether he was hospitalized in the service; an 1889 inquiry mentions admissions at Roanoke Island and New Bern but no records for the North Carolina volunteers were found. Chronic bronchitis was the diagnosis in Jonathan's second hospitalization in May 1864. Appie Williford, fifty-two years old, first filed a widow's claim for pension on January 19, 1884. It states that she is the former Appie Johnson, who married Jonathan Williford on January 18, 1850 at the residence of Littleton Johnson. By 1884 only three of their five children were alive: Joseph John, born 1856, George D. born 1859, and James R., born 1862. John Hughes was one of the witnesses to Appie's pension application. His first wife Mary Eliza Williford had died in 1888 and he was now remarried but remained financially involved with the Willifords because his three children were heirs of their grandmother Appie. Jonathan's cause of death was lung disease, with bronchitis and consumption both mentioned in the records. The pension was initially rejected on July 25, 1890 in a letter that gives the date of Jonathan's death as May 9, 1870. In contradiction to the application, the declaration of pension gives his and Appie's wedding date as January 14, 1849.

Joseph H. Hunter, Appie's lawyer in Washington, D.C., collected affidavits in support of the application from individuals who had known Jonathan before, during, and after his military service. Much of the wording is similar in all the applications, so I reproduce in full Josiah Dunlow's for its wealth of personal detail and comment on highlights of the rest. When this affidavit was taken on May 25, 1889, Josiah was 49 years old. He stated:

> I knew Jonathan Williford the soldier from early boyhood. I was raised six or seven miles from him. He lived immediately on the public road to and near Windsor. I went very frequently to Windsor and rarely passed without seeing him. I think I

averaged seeing him once a week since the war until his death. We were members of the same church. I was intimately acquainted with him and his family before and after the war...saw him and was with him a great deal after the consolidation [of regiments 1 and 2]. I know that for several months before his discharge he was in a low state of health and was in the hospital much of the time and was in bad health when discharged. His health remained bad after reaching home. He was never well afterward, though he was able to be up and do some work. He would have occasional attacks and get down low and then grow better and go out again. For several months before his death he broke completely down and never got out again. He had consumption, and I verily believe he contracted it in the army for he was a strong sound man when he enlisted and was in bad health before and after his discharge and continued so until he died.

Reporting more or less the same details was J. M. Butler, 59, who said that he and Jonathan were raised in the same neighborhood, went to school together, and knew each other during the war. Calling Jonathan "a very poor man" unable to pay a doctor, Butler mentions that he was twice married, the first time in 1847 without issue.

Appie Williford's affidavit is rich in details. Although she and Jonathan were Baptists, they had not had their children baptized. Elizabeth Carter, sixty-one years old in 1889, had been living with the Willifords when Appie's children were born, and provided an affidavit in proof of the children's dates of birth. In it, she states that William had died "about the year 1875" and that Mary Eliza died in 1888. (In 1884, Carter had given William's date of death as 9 May 1877.) She named Jonathan's first wife as

Margaret Johnson and said that they had married in 1847, but she died only 10 months from the wedding. Among the affidavits collected in 1891 to prove Appie's identity as Jonathan's widow was one by John R. Johnson, next-younger brother of Marcus. He and L.E. Butler testified that they had known Jonathan and Appie all their lives, as they were born and raised within a mile of them. On December 5, 1891, Marcus provided an affidavit which reveals that Jonathan's "first wife was sister of his last wife" and died "before the war." Marcus reported that Appie is "very poor" but "has a dower interest in a small piece of land which I don't believe yields her more than ten ($10.00) a year income." Appie was feeble and in poor health, with a "very scanty support" from her farm and no property "except a little household plunder." Marcus concludes that he has never lived more than two and a half miles from them. John R.'s affidavit estimates the value of Appie's "household plunder" at no more than $25. Their brother Haywood also submitted an affidavit, and echoes most of the details in the other affidavits. He describes Jonathan as a "stout muscular sound man" before the war adding that "for a year or so after his action he could work part of the time but for about two years before his death he was unable to labor" although he was a "most industrious man." Haywood concludes "I am positive that he contracted his disease while in the army."

At the end of her life, Appie's poverty was relieved by a widow's pension, in the amount of eight dollars per month starting May 9, 1870 and twelve dollars per month from March 1886. Had the pension been awarded when she first applied, the poverty of her later years would have been greatly alleviated. But she was so close to death when it was finally approved that her children benefited far more than she did. Each of the three surviving sons was allowed two dollars per month from the date of their father's death through his sixteenth birthday. Each son wrote a report after Appie's death, when there was confusion about the handling of the pensions by Windsor lawyer C. T. Harden. In a letter to the Commissioner of Pensions in Washington, Special Examiner E. T. Whitcomb concluded that Harden had mishandled two hundred dollars of Appie's funds but as these were now deposited into an account for the heirs, no charges were recommended. Each of the three sons had received two hundred dollars outright, and ex-son-in-law John Hughes was given one hundred. The sons believed the pension amount to be around $2400, whereas it was actually $2700. George Williford's affidavit explains that Mr. Duncan Winston of Windsor first asked George to bring his mother to town to discuss the pension to which she was entitled. He understood that Harden had received six hundred dollars from Appie, but three hundred of it was a loan which he repaid at the time of her death, February 3, 1893. Harden "came into the case after not know what became of the remaining three hundred dollars but had heard that the widow of Mr. Winston received one hundred at the instructions of Mrs. Williford. Son James testified in his affidavit that Winston died before the pension was approved, and his mother asked him to take her to Harden to discuss pursuing the application. Neither son knew any details of a payment agreement. The check arrived in August 1892, six months before Appie's death. James said the family had a general understanding that Harden was to be paid two hundred dollars for his assistance. Her third son Joseph John explained in his affidavit how his mother obtained the services of a Washington, D.C. lawyer: "I saw an advt. In the paper or on a poster which had Joseph H. Hunter's name to it, to the effect that widows of soldiers could get pensions. And I told her about it."

None of the three sons objected to Harden receiving

two hundred dollars for his labors, but the lawyer's affidavit revealed something that Appie had kept from them. "The amount was over $2700—I think. While I was there she told me she wanted to give Cora (a supposed illegitimate child she had raised whose other name is unknown to me) $300. No one was present but Cora and I and the pensioner. She took me to one side and asked me to withhold $300 from the knowledge of the sons above named. . . the sons were opposed to her giving Cora any, and she didn't want them to know anything about it until after she was dead as she didn't expect to live long."

Appie Johnson Williford, 1830-1893

Chapter 3
Planters' Sons

450,000 Union troops came from slave states in the South, especially border states, half as many as fought for the Confederacy.[1] William W. Freehling concludes that "If the North had won without anti-Confederate Southerners' reinforcements, victory would have come harder and taken longer."[2] Freehling's *The South vs. The South* takes on the myth of the solidly Confederate South, exploring the divisions within the region that contributed to Union victory. The case of Bertie County, almost evenly divided between Confederates and Unionists, was far from unusual.

No Johnson or Johnston appears as a slaveholder in the 1850 and 1860 slave censuses of Bertie County. Sometime during the 1850s, Josiah's father Elmore Dunlow had acquired one slave, a seventy-year-old man. Their relationship was in no way typical of plantation life, just two old men working twenty-two acres together. The Union allegiance of the Johnsons and Dunlows was clearly rooted in their position in the class structure. Josiah's brief AWOL period and Marcus's extended desertion suggest that they were less than honorable soldiers for the Union. The fact that Marcus and Littleton Johnson were among the many who first signed up for Confederate army service, and then quickly deserted, renders the Johnson family legacy less than heroic. So the urge to glorify one's ancestors' war records is frustrated in these cases by inconvenient facts.

Jonathan Williford, however, seems a more plausible candidate for heroism. Born into plantation society, he fought for the Union honorably and admirably. No desertion mars his record, and he returned to service in the most harrowing conditions imaginable after the debacle at Plymouth. Jonathan's life story illustrates the fluidity of class in the antebellum South. As the youngest son of a major plantation owner, Jonathan ended up living on two hundred acres of land at the southern end of the Pell Mell Pocosin, married to a Johnson. His father John Williford had owned more than five thousand acres of much better land adjacent to Beaver Dam Swamp in the north end of Bertie County. How did he fall so far as to fight for the Union alongside his Johnson in-laws against the plantation system that had nurtured him?

    A Williford family history helps situate Jonathan in time and place. Unlike the Johnsons and Dunlows, who present genealogical "brick walls" in the late eighteenth century, the Willifords have inspired a family history that traces their origin as far back as seventeenth century England. The first Williford to arrive in Bertie County was Richard, who first appears in county documents in 1717 witnessing a deed. In May 1723 he bought two hundred acres on "Quakeson swamp" and the following year he added another hundred acres on "Ahotskey Swamp," both now in Hertford County. He continues to appear in Bertie land transaction records through 1764, and in 1766 his son Richard was ordered by the County Court to administer his estate. His land was divided in 1769 among his three sons Richard, Benton, and John. In 1764 he had given Benton "my plantation and all lands that belong to me on the western side of Old Cashy and personal property also." The same year John was given one hundred fifty acres in Beaverdam Swamp at the site of a bridge. John left Bertie for Hertford County around 1768, and two years later Benton also left the county. Richard Jr. was the only son to remain in Bertie, where he died in 1808. In 1800 Richard Jr. was listed as owner of 1700 acres, but this was after making several deeds of gift to family members during the previous two decades. His two sons Abner and John are the ancestors of all the many subsequent Willifords in Bertie.

They both received gifts of 250 acres on Beaver Dam Swamp in the early 1780s, and John was given another hundred acres in 1799 adjacent to the "Askew line." Richard Williford's 1808 will names John his executor, gives him six slaves and the remainder of the estate not assigned to his other children, none of whom received land. Both sons increased their land holdings over the years, and by 1810 John was taxable for 3598 acres, all in the Beaver Dam Swamp area. John Williford's 1833 will is testimony to the considerable wealth he accumulated, but also to the lingering effects of primogeniture as a de facto practice long after it was abolished as law. John's oldest son William received 800 acres, and his widow Polly (Mary) was given the rest of his land and four slaves. The youngest sons Richard and John were left only two slaves each, while second son Jethro received a hundred dollars. Daughters Sarah, Mary, Nancy, Adaline, Elizabeth, and Ophelia (the only one unmarried at the time of John's death) each received comparably small amounts of money or numbers of slaves. Although the will ordained that John was to receive the home and land on which the family lived, known the Thomas Cook Plantation, at the time of his mother's death, this did not in fact occur. Her estate papers, dated 21 May 1841, show that her son-in-law Asa Early was executor and the estate sale netted just $36.69. John appears as purchaser of a bed and bolster, a chest, and a large trunk. The fate of the plantation on which Mary had lived is unclear from deed books, but it did not pass to John. He was however given a large share of the income from the hiring out of slaves to neighbors. He was paid $15 for the labor of "negroes Penny and two children" from May 21, 1841 through the following January 1.

The youngest son John was known throughout most of his life as Jonathan, and several documents indicate the transition. The only deed involving him on record is an 1847 purchase of 200 acres from Joshua Mizell for $250. This land was adjacent to Will's Quarter Swamp and Licking Branch on the road from Colerain to Windsor. Now known as the Bull Hill Road, this marks the southern boundary of the Pell Mell Pocosin. Here Jonathan resided for the rest of his life. The purchaser's name was originally written as John Wilford, but "than" was written in another ink after "John" each time it appeared. How could someone whose father intended that he inherit a large plantation and several slaves end up with a much smaller parcel of land in a more marginal area? The fact that an older brother-in-law was executor of Polly's estate might have influenced this development, which was not unusual in the plantation South. In *The Mind of the South*, W. J. Cash points out that in any large plantation family some members would end up as Jonathan Williford did: "Given a dozen cousins—brothers, if you wish, one or two would carve out plantations at home. . . another or two, migrating westward, might be lucky enough to do the same thing there; four or five, perhaps attempting the same goal, would make just enough headway to succeed as yeoman farmers; and the rest would. . . gradually be edged back to poorer and poorer lands. In the end, they—or the weakest and least competent of their sons—would have drifted back the whole way; would definitely have joined the ranks of the crackers. And once there, they would be more or less promptly and more or less fully forgot- ten by their more prosperous kinsmen."[6] Cash defines the poor whites as "the weakest elements of the old backcountry population. . . who had been driven back farthest. . . to all the marginal lands of the South; those who, because of the poorness of the soil on which they dwelt or the great inaccessibility of markets, were, as a group, most completely barred off from escape or economic or social advance."[7] Settling in the Pell Mell Pocosin and marrying a Johnson was a clear indication that Jonathan Williford had "drifted back the whole way" from the planter status of his father to poverty. He had become a Pell Meller, and this marked him as being on the bottom rung of white society in the county.

John Hughes was without doubt a Pell Meller, born and raised in the heart of the pocosin region to a mother whose family had been living there for several generations. Ludie Hughes was the daughter of Henry Hughes and Charlotte White, neighbors of John Butler and Charney Cale. Henry Hughes was the son of Charles Hughes and Sarah Mott, both of whom are brick walls for genealogists. Henry first appears in Bertie records in March 1818, buying sixty-five acres from Jesse Halsey for $100. The land bordered Marvel Swamp and neighbors Reuben Harrison, William Newborn, and John Butler. Almost thirty years later in July 1847, Henry Hughes made a gift tohis son Levi of forty- two and a half acres. This land was adjacent to Marvel Swamp, bordered by that of William Butler and Charney Cale. Since William would have inherited neighboring land from his father John Butler, it appears that this acreage is part of the original sixty-five acres Henry Hughes purchased in 1818. At the same time, Henry gave his son Miles Hughes another forty-two and a half acres in the same locale, so he had apparently owned at least eighty-five acres in total. By 1850 Henry had disappeared from the census, so presumably his transfer of land was in anticipation of approaching death.

Ludie was the subject of a bastardy bond dated February 12, 1844. Signed by her brother Levi and James Cherry, the bond required the payment of one hundred pounds to Bertie County. This obligation was void "if the aforesaid Ludy Hughes Levi Hughes & James Cherry...at all times hereafter acquit discharge & save harmless the county aforesaid and inhabitants of the state aforesaid from all costs charges and trouble whatsoever for and by means of the birth maintenance of and bringing up of the said child and of & from all suits charges & demands whatsoever touching and concerning the same." James Cherry might be considered a likely father of the child since he signed the bastardy bond, but several pieces of evidence point to another man as John's father. An online query I posted about John's parentage produced a reply saying that because he named his son Wiley Askew Hughes, John's father was probably Wiley Askew. Although he was one of the richest planters in the county, Wiley has been very elusive as a research subject. Online genealogical information on the Askews of Bertie County is abundant, but no one has identified Wiley's parents. Searching through deeds and wills and census records I was perplexed at how such a wealthy man could be so difficult to trace. But he is still a "brick wall" for whom even deeds are rare. Tax lists from the 1820s consistently list Wiley's name next to that of Justin Askew as owners of slaves but no real estate. They were presumably brothers and minor heirs, but no will has been found leaving them slaves.

The first deed in Wiley's name appears in 1831, followed by additional purchases in 1832 and 1837. As of the 1850 census, six-year-old John Hughes resided with his grandmother Charlotte, his aunt Martha Hughes, and six-month-old Levi Johnston. The column for land value is left blank on the census form, so presumably the house was on land owned by another relative. Wiley Askew was living with his wife Eliza, three sons Thomas, William, and Benjamin, and twenty-two slaves on a farm valued at $4500. But Eliza died during the 1850s, and in 1857 Wiley made a very fortunate second marriage to Mary Gill, daughter of a neighboring planter. The same year his son Thomas married Mary's younger sister Ann Eliza Gill. In November 1857, the month of his second marriage, "Willie" Askew was appointed patroller in the Cashie

Neck. The 1860 census shows Wiley and Mary owning forty-three slaves, with $11,000 in real estate and $36,665 in personal property. Alliance with the Gill family was equally fortunate for Thomas's finances, as in 1860 he owned $9,000 in real estate and $21,680 in personal property. The February 1856 County Court apprenticed John Hughes, "orphan, aged around 11" to his uncle Levi Hughes. Since both of his parents were alive, although not married to each other, calling him an orphan was literally inaccurate although perhaps appropriate as a measure of his social status.

Gerald Thomas devoted many years to documenting the Civil War history of the county, resulting eventually in two books that explore the deep divisions in Bertie. *Bertie in Blue* focuses entirely on the Union soldiers' war experiences, but his first book, *Divided Loyalties*, devotes equal attention to the Confederates. The Confederate company in which John Hughes served was created as part of a light artillery battalion commanded by Solomon H. Whyte. In May 1862 its members were transferred to infantry service and assigned as Company G of the Thirty-Second Regiment North Carolina troops.[12] When John Hughes enrolled on April 1, 1862 he gave his age as nineteen. His first muster roll shows him to have been sick in camp, but thereafter his military career was fairly uneventful until Gettysburg. John was 5' 7" with gray eyes and a dark complexion, according to his military records. Company G was stationed near Drewry's Bluff, Virginia at the time John enlisted with many other Bertie County men, and remained there until the end of the year. The company was stationed near Kinston, North Carolina for the first four months of 1863, but during May and June it was moving towards Pennsylvania. John's muster roll for July and August 1863 notes that he was wounded and taken prisoner at Gettysburg on July 2. That is his last appearance in

Confederate records, but at this point he enters the rolls of prisoners of war held by the Union army. After being hospitalized in several federal hospitals, on October 16, 1863, he was admitted to the USA General Hospital at West's Buildings in Baltimore with the complaint of "debility." He is on a roll of prisoners who were transferred from Baltimore on November 12, 1863 to City Point, Virginia as part of a group of 350 Confederate prisoners. Company records do not indicate his returning to duty, but he must have done so, since on July 26, 1864, John deserted and came into Federal lines at Roanoke Island.

John married Mary Eliza Williford on March 24,1871, less than a year after her father died. The 1880 census shows them with four children: Wiley, Martha, Mary, and William. Also in the household is Kitty Dempsey, a white female house servant of twenty-seven. Mary Eliza was also twenty- seven, her husband ten years older. Because John named his firstborn son after Wiley Askew, it would appear that there was an acknowledgment of his kinship with the Askews. Although the firstborn legitimate son was successful from the point of view of financial resources, his life does not appear to have been a happy one. Thomas Askew was documented by the county court system more than any other member of any of my ancestral families in the late nineteenth century.

In 1855 Thomas R. Askew successfully sued Thomas Holley and was awarded $52.50 and costs. In the fall of 1873, Thomas was fined fifty dollars after a suit by Jacob Pruden. In the spring of 1878, Thomas pled guilty to a charge unspecified in the court minutes and paid costs, with judgment suspended. Eighteen months later, Thomas sued F. C. Miller, but the jury awarded $2616.80 for the defendant. In 1884 perhaps anticipating his demise, Thomas sold his twenty-two-year-old son Wiley G. Askew

164 acres for $1312. Court records show that in the fall of 1885, Thomas R. Askew's children, with no suitable guardians, were deemed orphans by the court. The final report in his estate papers show that his property was valued at $11709.73, of which $9362.62 had been paid to creditors by April 1887.

Thomas R. Askew's next younger brother William L. served as executor of his estate, but he also died before their father Wiley. In lieu of an estate record, there is a report by the Superior Court clerk W. L. Lyon dated July 31, 1891, stating that Wiley died intestate with an estate valued at seventy-five dollars and that heirs Thomas R. and W. L. Askew were deceased. On May 23, 1892, the year after Wiley Askew died, the Atlanta newspaper reported: "A Special tonight says a cyclone swept through Bertie county wrecking all the houses on Wiley Askews farm. It leveled the trees on William Pritchards place. Some of these fell on his house and crushed it, killing one of his children instantly and breaking the other's back."[15]

In the Spring 1890 session of Superior Court, the State on behalf of Willie H. Askew and Maggie A. Askew, sued Wiley G. Askew and A. J. Holloman, administrator of W. L. Askew, dec'd, the result being $999.41 and an additional $1273.36 provided for Thomas's younger children, plus $25 to lawyers.

In 1890, John Hughes bought forty acres of land for $130 from his former in-law William Williford and his wife. In February 1894, Hughes signed a paper accepting his responsibilities as legal guardian of his children Mary L. Hughes, William C. Hughes, John N. Hughes, Lillie M. Media Hughes, as well as Martha Perry. (Wiley was no longer a minor at this point.) All are called minor heirs of Apply Williford, their grandmother. Among the responsibilities were to take charge of their estate and make annual settlements. On August 30, 1888 John married Manessa (Millie) Cowand by whom he had two sons, Grover and Horace. After her death he married Carrie Askew Perry on December 6, 1904, and lived with her just over nine years until his own death in January 1914.

The destruction of Wiley Askew's farm by a tornado confirmed the fall of the house of Askew already accomplished by the poverty and deaths of Wiley, Thomas, and William. What had been one of the wealthiest families in the county had suffered huge losses. But the illegitimate son and half-brother John Hughes outlived his Askew family for twenty years and carried on his father's legacy by naming his son Wiley Askew Hughes. This choice would seem to be an open acknowledgment of his own illegitimacy. How did John Hughes relate to Thomas and William Askew as older half-brothers? One can readily surmise that these kinship ties were not discussed with outsiders, but within the family such questions were bound to arise. All the documentary evidence is in favor of the premise that the kinship ties were openly and mutually acknowledged in both these cases. John Hughes had many more White than Askew half-siblings through his mother Ludie and her husband William White. Their daughter Nancy White married Josiah Dunlow, making Josiah and John half-brothers in law. The two men, who had fought on opposite sides in the Civil War, were lifelong friends by the evidence of legal documents. But I found no evidence about whether the kinship between John Hughes and his half-sister Nancy Dunlow was openly acknowledged in the family and neighborhood.

John Hughes had no full siblings, and was defined as an orphan in a legal document when both parents were alive and taking care of their legitimate offspring. John's half-siblings through his mothers were Whites, Pell Mellers through and through, as poor as the Butlers, Dunlows and Johnsons living along the road to Ross Church. But his Askew father and half-brothers had been among the richest men in the county, in a family doomed to lose all its wealth. Most of the people in the area who carried the Askew name were former slaves, a constant reminder to the white Askews of their former estate.

William Fred Johnson, 1901-1937

Chapter 4

Class War

Bertie County was atypical among North Carolina counties in that slaves outnumbered whites by a significant margin in 1860. Planters, defined as owning at least twenty slaves, were only an eighth of all slaveholders in the state. In Bertie County, however, that proportion was almost one-fifth. In the state as a whole seventy-two percent of the white families owned no slaves, but in Bertie County the figure was sixty-one percent. Bertie was close to the state average in farm sizes with just over forty-five percent of farms containing fewer than fifty acres, compared to forty-two percent statewide in 1860. More than sixty-five percent of Bertie farms contained fewer than a hundred acres, compared to more than sixty-nine percent statewide.

Although more than two thirds of white farmers in the state owned no slaves in 1860, North Carolina's General Assembly had the highest slaveholder proportion of any state legislature in the South, exceeding eighty-five percent. Even before the Civil War, poor whites were seen as a threat by the planter class. In 1857, voters approved free suffrage of white males by a greater than two-to-one margin, and thereafter the elite was constantly fighting to retain its privileged position. Most farmers owned between three and six hundred dollars each of real and personal property. As conditions worsened during the war, yeomen found their former self-sufficient life unsustainable, which caused the state to lead the Confederacy in desertions as well as other measures of dissatisfaction. The rapid decline in living conditions was shocking, and yeomen felt that "conditions had become intolerable, and they had lost their social autonomy."[1] Buffaloes acted with particular hostility toward the rich, Escott reports. In Tyrrell County it was claimed by a Confederate sympathizer that "Buffaloe houses all around the country are supplied with books & furniture taken fr. Houses of loyal citizens who have come away."[2]

An interesting story about the reason one Hertford County soldier gave for fighting in the Union army was reported by a grandson. "Where I lived, there were people who didn't like us much better than the Negroes, and I kind of felt like that if they won, sooner or later they would buy and sell us, too."[3] In light of the history of Indian slavery in Bertie County, people with mixed Native ancestry had every reason to share the fear voiced by Isaac Pearce. But even poor whites of purely European ancestry (presumably including Pearce) were aware that their class interests were incompatible with those of the Confederacy.

In *Common Whites*, historian Bill Cecil-Fronsman notes that North Carolina slaves and planters have both received far more scholarly attention that the poor whites who outnumbered both. He attempts to explain "the extent of common-white class consciousness and the factors that prevented it from developing further."[4] Because poor whites frequently confronted the planters, Cecil-Fronsman is skeptical of the hegemony theory which argues that planters had convinced common folk that the social order was fair.

In 1860 only 9100 of roughly 35,000 North Carolina slave- holders, fewer than eight percent of all whites, owned ten or more slaves, while more than seventy percent of whites owned none. In 1850, almost half of the state legislators had owned no slaves, although within ten years the non-slaveholders were down to fifteen percent. One study found that marriages between non-slaveowners and owners of fewer than ten slaves were not unusual, but those who owned ten or more slaves married almost entirely within their own class. The folklore of common whites included stories and songs with the message that love can overcome distinctions of wealth and class, but "these maxims were not always heeded."[5] The definition of "common white" varied from one locality to another; an owner of nine slaves in Halifax County might be considered common because such a large percentage of whites there, more than fourteen percent, owned ten or more.

The land transactions of Marcus Johnson indicate the financial pressures under which poor whites in Bertie struggled in the postwar era. In 1870, Marcus bought 109 acres from R. E. Bazemore and his wife, taking out a mortgage with Andrew Craig and John Gilliam. After 1879, Marcus was involved in many more sales or mortgages than purchases of land. He took out a mortgage with Darby Overton in 1879, and sold timber rights to Greenleaf Johnson in 1880, to Branch Goode in 1881, and to Lekies and Collins in 1882. The same year, Marcus sold the Public School Committee an acre of land for a school site (perhaps the present site of Bertie County High School, across the road from the Johnson homeplace). In 1887 he took out a mortgage with H. W. Lyon on the 109 acres he had purchased from the Bazemores and paid the earlier mortgage to Craig and Gilliam. Three years later, he paid off the mortgage to banker Lyon, and there were no more mortgages after 1890. He sold small parcels to John C. Baker and John Hughes in 1883, to Martha J. Cherry in 1887, to Sam Overton in 1889; to William Williford and others in 1889 jointly with D. Overton; to W. M. Keeter in 1890; and again to the Public School Committee in 1890 (jointly with his neighbor John Hughes); to Thomas Askew in 1891; and to George E. Byrd 1893. While these transactions individually were minor, the overall trend was clearly a steady loss of acreage over a twenty-year period. The fact that all his sons left Bertie County around the turn of the century is further indication of hard times for the family.

The Windsor newspaper in the late 1880s recorded the county commissioners' expenditures every month and included a list of people who got "help outside the poorhouse." Winnie Dunlow was in every monthly list receiving two dollars; on a couple of occasions her sister Polly Butler received three. Polly's sister-in-law Abby Butler was in several monthly lists, receiving ten dollars each time. These stipends, the equivalent of welfare, were received by a few dozen people each month. Pell Mellers did not seem to be over- or under-represented among the county's recipients of such aid.

The colonial slave code of 1715 had been designed to prevent excessive familiarity between the races, and successfully promoted racism on the part of poor whites. Emancipation was opposed almost unanimously by common whites, who generally shared the elite's disdain for blacks, yet sometimes assisted runaway slaves. Cecil-Fronsman points out that there was more contact between the races than has been recognized in the first third of the nineteenth century, since "7.5% of divorces in North Carolina were granted for cohabitation with blacks."[6] A recent academic thesis has analyzed the evidence concerning the reasons that North Carolinians chose to fight for the Union in the Buffalo regiments. Judkin Jay Browning was a graduate student in history when he became interested in this topic, which had received little analysis in earlier descriptive studies. Browning offers four competing explanations of the name Buffaloes and how it came to be applied to the First and Second Infantries.[7]

John A. Hedrick, a Confederate sympathizer, wrote in an October 1862 letter that "their uniforms make them appear so large that the people call them 'buffaloes'" and "they go around in gangs like herds of buffaloes." The noun buffle meant a fool or fathead, or "one who knowingly takes false oaths for money." As a verb 'buffalo' meant to "bamboozle, be-wilder, overawe, baffle." Browning combines several definitions in one, concluding that, "Confederates perceived as fools those rebel turncoats who employed deceit and treachery in swearing an oath of allegiance to the Union or enlisting in the Federal army for the bounty money."[8] There was a faction of a third party in the 1837 elections in New York City called Buffaloes. Finally, before the fall of Roanoke Island, local rebels told blacks that Yankees had horns growing out of their foreheads. The last two accounts seem highly unlikely as explanations, and Browning's combination of the rest suffices as a plausible reconstruction. Unlike typical regiments of the Civil War, the First and Second North Carolina Infantries did not have companies marching together and acting as one unit, because they never were present at a single location. The total strength of the First was almost 1050 men by the end of the war, after the two were consolidated. Charles Henry Foster, who had been a newspaper editor in Murfreesboro before the war, received a captain's commission to recruit the Second in August 1862, but only succeeded in raising five companies, half the usual number. About one hundred of the 350 members of the Second were "turncoats," Confederate deserters, including company commander Littleton Johnson. 3200 white North Carolinians served in the Union army, but only the 1400 from the eastern part of the state were called Buffaloes. Fifteen percent of the Buffaloes had deserted from the Confederate army. Black North Carolina Union soldiers outnumbered whites, with a total enrollment estimated at 5035. Judson Browning corroborates Branch's report that they were held in contempt by North Carolinians throughout the twentieth century. Yet for the latter third of the nineteenth century, the Roanoke Valley witnessed a remarkable transformation, becoming the center of Republican political power in the state and a unique example of interracial political allegiances. In the 1880s and 90s, Bertie County was part of the Second Congressional District, called the "Black Second" because most Republican voters were black and the district was solidly Republican. In a study of the district, Eric Anderson analyzes the social changes that followed the war. In 1870, the number of farms in the district with five hundred or more acres in cultivation had declined by more than seventy percent from 1860 levels. At the same time, there was a large increase in the total number of farms; 198 percent in the two decades between 1860 and 1880. Sharecropping accounted for about two thirds of the farm labor in the district, but Bertie County farms were always disproportionately owner occupied.

In 1874 a Democrat newspaper editor in the district wrote that scalawags (southern whites allied with blacks and northerners) were lower in his preference than carpetbaggers or Negroes. This reflects prewar class antagonisms that had become magnified by the political alliances of the postwar era. Voters in the second district biennial election during the Reconstruction era, showing that black political participation was not disruptive to competitiveness in the democratic process. In 1874 a former slave from Bertie, George Mebane, was elected to the state senate representing the third district. Most Republican voters were black in 1880 as in all other elections of the era, but a substantial minority of Bertie County whites were active in the Republican party.

Francis D. Winston, the lawyer who handled most legal transactions for the Johnsons and Dunlows, was on the Liberal-Republican ticket as Superintendent of Public Instruction in 1884. In 1888, he was elected as a Republican to the state senate to represent Bertie and Northampton. But the era of interracial cooperation in Bertie politics ended after 1890, when former Republican strongholds became competitive for Democrats. In 1890, Francis Winston left the Republican Party citing national issues, although he continued to call himself "a friend of the Negro."[9] Two years later another major Bertie Republican defected when Clerk of Court William L. Lyon announced that he would vote for Grover Cleveland and all other Democratic candidates in the 1892 election, and denounced the Republicans in a letter to the *Windsor Ledger*:

> The party as conducted in Eastern North Carolina has become a byword and reproach. Their conventions have become howling mobs and nominations are put up to the highest bidder. Ignorant, incompetent, and corrupt Negroes have taken complete control of the political machinery and have nominated for positions of profit, honor, and trust most incompetent and corrupt men, while men of respectability who served the party faithfully for years are allowed no voice in the deliberations of the party. They have driven away from the party nearly every white Republican and hundreds of the best colored people are disgusted. I can no longer stay with a party managed by such men.[10]

After the 1892 election, the *Windsor Ledger* assured the black citizens of Bertie County that they would not be harmed by the triumph of the Democrats, many of whom had received black support. By 1894, the Republican party in the second district had experienced a steady decline in power since 1887, but although "weakened and disorganized" it was "still a biracial organization in an increasingly segregated society."[11] The Populist movement had been gaining strength for several years by 1894 when it adopted the tactic of "fusion" with Republicans to take control of the legislature. The 1896 election showed the results of this winning combination, as changes in election law enabled Republicans to elect a black congressman, making North Carolina unique in the South in its level of black political representation. In 1898 Bertie had sixteen black magistrates and nine black postmasters thanks to the liberalized election laws of the fusion legislature. Anderson concludes, "Judged by the standards of the nineteenth-century South, the legal system allowed a remarkable degree of black participation, especially in the Second Judicial District."[12] The last black congressman to serve for many years to come, George C. White was reelected to a second and final term in 1898. In that year, Democrats swept back into power through race-baiting, "Negro domination" being the bogeyman used to bring poor whites back into line.

Fraud and intimidation secured the passage of a 1900 constitution that all but disenfranchised blacks in the state. In some counties, Democratic vote totals outnumbered the total white population. Intimidation tactics were directed at black voters, as for example in Bertie's Snakebite township where several were disenfranchised for not knowing their birth dates. Reviewing the *Windsor Ledger* for the crucial election year 1898, I found no immediate family members of my ancestors involved in politics that year. All but one of the distant cousins who are identifiable in the political news were on the Fusion side. In the first editorial of the year, editor Stephen W. Kenney wrote that "those who stand in the way of Democratic resurgence are traitors to the race" while welcoming former Populists and Republicans to join that resurgence. Later editorials denounced governor Daniel Russell, claiming that Democrats were "fighting for white people" and "can protect white womanhood."[13] In September, the

Ledger editorialized that Wilmington had become "completely negroized" and denounced a black newspaper editor there who had become the scapegoat for white race riots that brought Democratic rule to the city.[14] The Johnsons' neighbor Levin Butler was active in Bertie Democratic politics that year, and Littleton's son Walter R. Johnson also appeared among their faction. Among the Republicans, Clerk of Court candidate G.W. Mizell (also listed as W.G.) won 1774 votes but was defeated by William Lyon, the newly-converted Democrat, with 1895 votes. Frank Cale had been a white Republican candidate for county commissioner but withdrew before the election. In the first edition after the election, the *Ledger* printed huge headlines reading "Hurrah North Carolina is Saved" and stories inside headed "Democracy's Glorious Day" and "White People Take Charge of Bertie County."[15]

In his memoir *It's a Far Country*, Patrick Winston described Windsor in the late nineteenth century as a place where political polarization was extreme and violence was a common occurrence:

> Every Saturday was a full holiday for the farmers. On that day the vacant lots, the hotel stables and other available spaces would be filled with whinnying horses and braying jacks. By twelve o'clock half the visitors would be comfortably drunk, the Democrats with liquor from Skriven's bar on King Street, the Republicans and negroes from whiskey from Sheriff Bell's groggery on Granville Street. Presently a dispute would arise between the fighting Caspers and Whites and Dundelowes. The lie would pass and the cry would go up, 'Fight, fight!' Everyone would prick up his ears and rush to the scene of the battle, where a dozen men were knocking, scratching and biting one another with

great impartiality. To miss a part in the free-for-all fight was considered a sore disappointment.[16]

Anderson explains the social pressures on white Republicans and Populists in eastern North Carolina at this time: "Motivated by his fear of ostracism, his hatred of ruthless foes, his racial prejudice, his sense of order and purpose in history, he [the white fusion voter] was forced to make a decision as agonizing as the one that confronted the men of 1861."[17] Nowhere was the pressure on white Republicans greater than in the black belt counties where Fusion had been most successful, as "strident appeals to white solidarity put almost unbearable pressure on the party's white minority."[18] In the case of Bertie County, one possible result was massive emigration by Pell Mellers around the turn of the century.

Norfolk Riverside Cemetery photo courtesy of Joan Marie Revell

72

Johnson Graves in Riverside Cemetery, Norfolk
Photos courtesy of Carl Unterbrink

Chapter Five:
Johnson Reunions

Growing up in South Norfolk, I thought of it as a small Southern town. Only after leaving did I realize that it had the look and feel of a northeastern industrial suburb, rather than a typical rural Virginia town. Most people lived in two-story frame houses on 25-foot lots, crammed together so tightly as to be almost row houses. Yet South Norfolk was populated by rural Carolinians and Virginians one generation removed from the farm. The area developed between 1890 and 1920 to house working class migrants who came seeking jobs in the knitting mills, shipyards, and fertilizer factories along the Southern branch of the broad Elizabeth River. They came mostly from northeastern North Carolina, and one small area a few miles square was especially well represented. The Johnsons and the Dunlos came from a part of Bertie County which by that time was Askewville but had been known through most of the eighteenth and nineteenth centuries as the Pell Mell Pocosin, a huge peat bog covered with thick forests of longleaf pine. The pocosin's soil was so poorly drained that much of it remained uninhabitable until modern drainage systems were introduced. Surrounded by swamps that flowed into the Cashie and Chowan rivers, the pocosin (Algonquian for "swamp on a hill") was home to a few dozen families who practiced subsistence farming in patches of higher ground that had been cleared in the midst of the forest.In the South Norfolk public schools, I rubbed shoulders with Mizelles, Hoggards, Castellows, Cowands, and Perrys, whose parents and grandparents were Pell Mellers—the derisive name applied to the pocosin's residents by the elite in Windsor, the Bertie county seat. Reading the census records of 1920 and 1930, one finds distinctive Pell Meller family names on almost every block in South Norfolk.

First visit to the Johnson cemetery on Bull Hill Road

Few houses are located on that stretch of highway, lined with pine forests owned by international corporations, interspersed with a few patches of older mixed woods including that in which the Johnson cemetery was located. Hiking through a pocosin was a new and different experience, unlike either the coastal flatlands of my youth or the Piedmont hills where I now live. The terrain is by no means flat, as the elevation varies about fifty feet. Standing water appears in no particular pattern, just as frequently in the higher elevations as near the Will's Quarter Swamp which flows beside the cemetery. I followed the trail to the cemetery, visible from some distance because of the tall hardwoods. The graves of Marcus and Rutha Johnson occupied the center of the acre in which Hawkinses and Johnsons were buried in the late nineteenth and early twentieth centuries.

After a couple of false starts, I found the right trail out and emerged feeling as if this expedition had been a rite of initiation. Hiking in jungly terrain to the edge of the swamp and a haunted-looking cemetery had probably taken only three miles even including two wrong turns. But in one hour I had reconnected with my lost Johnson family roots symbolically by making this pilgrimage. By the end of the year I had joined three dozen Johnson cousins, all new acquaintances, on a hike to the cemetery through the forest. It was fortunate that they photographed the area as it was then, because the next time we returned after a reunion in 2003 it was to a bleak, treeless expanse stretching from the road to the swamp. The pine forest was gone. A few weeks after my first visit to Askewville, I returned to Bertie County en route to the Port o' Plymouth/Roanoke River Museum whose curator once owned the Johnson/Hawkins cemetery where my great-great grandparents are buried. This bright March day in 2001 was a fortunate one for my research. It started with a morning hike back into the Johnson/Hawkins cemetery with a local genealogist, recording information from the gravestones. Then I spent an hour in Plymouth talking with the museum's curator Harry Thompson, a leading Bertie County local historian, and finally ended up at the celebration of Askewville's fiftieth anniversary as an incorporated town. The afternoon event was held in the elementary school gymnasium where nearly a hundred people milled around looking at exhibits on local history. There were abundant historical photos and memorabilia associated with Johnsons and Dunlows on display. None of the local families has any conclusive identifications of specific Indian ancestors or their tribes, but many have oral traditions. All the local historians I encountered agreed that some area families have Indian ancestry, but there are different estimates of their prevalence and strength.

Three years of attending Dunlow and Johnson family reunions brought home the difference between one family that still had ownership of ancestral land and another that had lost it. The Johnson reunions were announced online by Mattieleene Johnson, wife of Marcus's great-grandson Charles, whose branch of the family had lived in the Rocky Mount area for more than a century. In November 2001, our first reunion was at a Baptist church in Ahoskie, followed by a hike to the Hawkins Johnson cemetery.

Ahoskie was founded in 1893, developing along a rail line that connected the county seats Winton and Windsor. The largest town in Hertford County, Ahoskie outgrew Windsor within twenty years of its founding. Hertford County's population growth and expanding industry made it a magnet for migrants from Bertie. The Johnson reunion in Ahoskie drew descendants of Marcus and his brothers from as far away as Illinois and Missouri, but most came from North Carolina and Virginia. The reunion was hosted by Marcus Wiley Johnson and his family and held in their Baptist church basement fellowship hall. After getting acquainted over a pot-luck dinner most of us proceeded down US 13 past the old home place to the family cemetery.

The old Johnson homeplace is now just a pile of ruins in a clearcut forest across from the county high school. The graves of Marcus and Rutha are a couple of miles east on what was once the farm of Marcus's younger brother John R. Johnson. Known as the Hawkins tract, it was sold by Harry Thompson to Champion International Paper Company with the agreement that the cemetery never be destroyed. Ownership has since been transferred to several other lumber companies but the tract remains timber land.

Downstream a couple of miles from the cemetery, Wills Quarter Swamp is dammed to form Hoggard's Mill Pond, near where Marcus and his brothers had grown up. After the cemetery tour was complete, Mattieleene and Charles invited me along for a brief visit to Viola Johnson White, whose granddaugghter Janine we knew from the Bertie Rootsweb site. Miss Viola and her family were descended from Hardy Hawkins Johnson, and none of us Marcus descendants had ever established how that branch of the family was connected to our own. We knew that Hardy Hawkins Johnson Jr. had served in the Federal Army in the same company C as Marcus, and that his family had lived near Askewville, but our kinship to him remains a mystery. I learned later that Miss Viola's father Perry Johnson bought the homeplace of Bun Dunlow in 1910, so she grew up in the house my own grandmother had left at the age of six.

Josiah Dunlow and Marcus Johnson served together in the First North Carolina Infantry, and were lifelong friends living a few miles apart. Both had thirteen children who survived into adulthood. Johnson and Dunlow arestill very common names in the Pell Mell region. But there was a huge difference between the histories of the two families. Almost all of Marcus's descendants left the county, and the reunion in Windsor didn't include a County resident who came from our line. It was all folks from Rocky Mount, or the Research Triangle, or Hampton Roads, or even Kansas City, piecing together the fragments of a family dispersed by the forces of history.

Returning to Johnson places was always an experience of emptiness and isolation, even though they are just past the outskirts of Windsor. The reunion group visiting the Johnson Hawkins cemetery was a collection of exiles remembering ghosts. The most haunting graves, and related stories, were the resting place of Maude Ruth Johnson Russell and her infant son James, who died in 1899 a year before his mother. Except for his youngest daughter Rockie, Marcus Johnson's children who survived into the twentieth century were unanimous in leaving the county. The places associated with him are not only out of family hands but long-abandoned and desolate. Yet they are on the edge of civilization in the form of a bustling county seat a few miles down-stream on the Cashie. Clearcutting of mature pines between Bull Hill Road and the Johnson cemetery has transformed a mystical journey through the forest into a dispiriting obstacle course through debris left behind by loggers. Nonetheless the riparian perimeter of Will's Quarter Swamp was left intact beyond the edge of the pocosin, so a few yards past the cemetery a line of trees secludes the still-magical cypress and tupelo swamp in its own private universe. The swamp and cemetery feel abandoned by the living but haunted by the dead, and you can easily imagine yourself a time traveler seeing the waterway as the Indians did.

Most of our direct Johnson ancestors lived

downstream along this swamp near the millpond at its confluence with the Cashie. The mill pond was the second place in Johnson family history I visited in 2001 after first seeing the cemetery, and the changes since then are far more benign than upstream. It continues to belong to Harry Thompson, and on a return trip I ran into him there in the company of two Nature Conservancy officials with whom he was discussing public access to the site. There isa quaint covered bridge at the approach to the millpond, which at first glance appears impossible to any craft. But allured by the challenge of kayaking where my ancestors milled their grain for decades, I put in and paddled a mile or so among the cypress knees where only a narrow channel could be discerned to follow upstream. Just a foot or two deep, the black water flowed with a definite current which was strongest at the mill site. According to legend, Marcus Johnson took a moonlit journey down the Cashie into the Federal army at Plymouth, which ultimately took him all the way to Fort Macon at the coast. His journey would likely have begun somewhere near Hoggard's Mill. A canoe in his father's estate indicates that the family land bordered a navigable stretch of Will's Quarter Swamp.

According to an 1840 deed, John Johnson bought land adjoining his own from Mills Cullipher, which hesold in 1845 to his brother Littleton. In 1846, Littleton Jr. acquired adjacent land that had belonged to William Hoggard, and was described as being on the south side of Hoggard's Mill Pond. The 1767 deed from Isaiah Johnson to his son John described the land as being on the south side of Will's Quarter Swamp, which later became Hoggard's Mill Creek, after the swamp was dammed to create the mill pond. So for several generations Johnsons lived along this waterway.

Apart from the two John Hawkins Johnson/Johnstons, there was only one John Johnston in Bertie's 1800 census, presumably the son of Isaiah and father of Littleton Sr. The latter, father of the John who died in 1861, bought land from Curry neighbors that was described as being on the same side of the same body of water. Hence our line of Bertie County Johnsons of the nineteenth century was probably a remnant branch of the Dobbs (now Lenoir) County Isaiah Johnson family whose sons went on to move further south. Johnsons married into a local Hawkins clan, as for example Marcus's sister Belinda who married William Hawkins. His grave on the edge of the Hawkins/Johnson cemetery is marked by a CSA tombstone, a few yards from Marcus's Union marker.

On Thanksgiving morning in 2004, I walked around Riverside Cemetery in Norfolk, looking for my great grandfather John Henry Johnson whose newspaper obituary claimed he was buried there. Although I never found him, his wife was listed in the cemetery index and Riverside was thick with the graves of Pell Mellers. First I found Oliver Dunlow, 1894-1934, and next to him his mother Luzann D. Gray 1869-1951. This is Aunt Lousanna (Louisiana, Luzan, etc.) oldest daughter of Josiah and Nancy Dunlow, who relocated with her second husband to South Norfolk and remarried there after his death. Right next to them were Pell Mellers Joseph Franklin Mizell,1883-1946 and Clara Kerman Mizell 1882-1934.

Just a few feet away was the big surprise, William Fred Johnson 1901-1937 "Beloved husband and father"— my grandfather whose grave I had never seen or heard mentioned before. Mary Hughes Johnson was listed in the cemetery index, but when I went to the gravesite it was unmarked, a measure perhaps of her family's poverty. Right next to her was the marked grave of her brother, Wiley Askew Hughes, 1872-1941, behind which were those of Wiley's son and daughter in law. Nearby were the graves of Mary's cousin George C. Williford, 1887-1974 and his wife Minnie E., 1886- 1973.

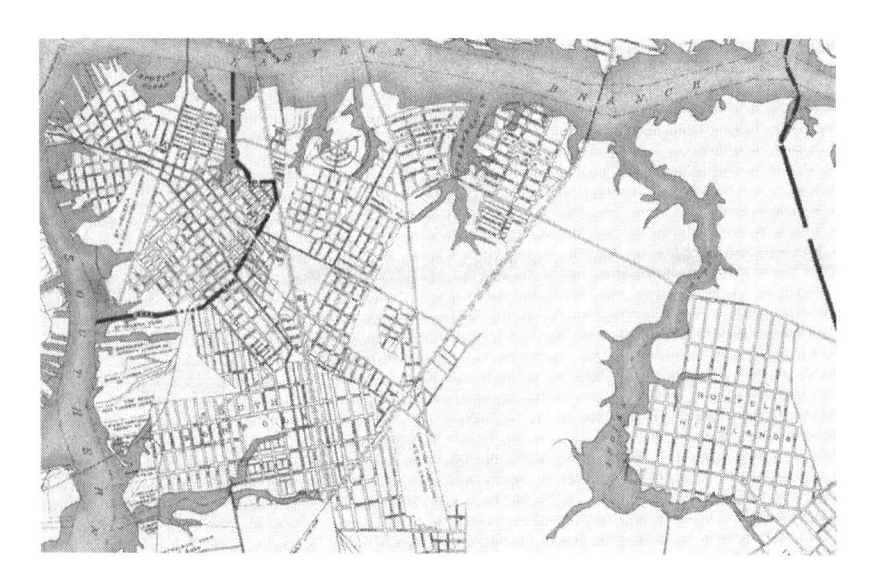

South Norfolk in 1921, when most Pell Mell migrants lived along Bainbridge Blvd. near the Southern Branch of the Elizabeth River on the left. Riverside Cemetery in the upper middle section is on the Eastern Branch at the top of the map.

Epilogue: In Search of the Dunlows

Dunlow Cemetery, Askewville

Genealogy is notoriously addictive, perhaps because each new discovery creates abundant new questions. During 2001, what began as a casual interest in family history rapidly escalated to an obsession with my paternal grandparents' birthplace, Bertie County. At the end of the year I bought a cabin in the Roanoke Valley of northeastern North Carolina, halfway between Bertie County and my job in Virginia. Over the next four years I visited Bertie County dozens of times, made frequent trips to the State Archives in Raleigh, and attended annual Dunlow (the Carolina spelling) and Johnson family reunions.

The region is haunted by its racial history as the former stronghold of plantation culture. Most of the North Carolina counties with slave majorities in 1860 were in the Roanoke Valley. Bertie was among them, as well as Warren County where I lived and Halifax which lies between; all retain African-American majorities today. This makes the Roanoke Valley a Democratic stronghold in a largely conservative state, but the region was a Republican enclave from the end of the Civil War until African Americans were disenfranchised in 1900.

Emancipation transformed the Roanoke Valley from the state's richest region to its poorest, as over half the population were no longer counted as valuable property of plantation owners but rather as penniless freedmen. The region has a high proportion of mobile homes compared to the rest of the state, often within sight of old houses in ruinous condition, "throwed away" in the terminology of eastern North Carolina. The five counties along the Roanoke were among the six with the lowest per capita incomes in 2000. Warren and Halifax, unlike Bertie, retain substantial Native American populations which is another distinctive feature of the Roanoke Valley that lured me to the region. Long marked by outmigration, Bertie led the state in population loss in the 1990s, the third consecutive decade of declining numbers. Its population density has fallen below 50 per square mile, less than a third the state average.

Bertie's physical environment alternates blessings and curses. The growing season exceeds 200 days, annual rainfall averages almost 50 inches, and there are fewer than six inches of annual snowfall. But the county has a relatively high frequency of tornadoes compared to other North Carolina counties, and is highly vulnerable to hurricanes and floods. The northern half of the county is forested by loblolly pine where once the longleaf was ubiquitous, and throughout the county tree farms dominate the landscape with over 70% of the land covered in forest. Nonetheless Bertie remains a state leader in corn, peanut and cotton production.

For almost twenty years I have paddled the rivers and streams of the Roanoke and Chowan basins, which converge in Bertie County. Once I began to explore genealogy I sought out waterways connected to family history and found an eerie consistency. The Cashie can be navigated only a mile or so above Windsor before tangles of downed trees in shallow water make further progress difficult if not impossible. Will's Quarter Swamp is dammed just above its confluence with the Cashie, creating a mill pond that can be paddled a half mile or so before one is stymied by log jams and shallows. Nearby, Cucklemaker Creek is entirely impassible where it once flowed deep enough to support canoe traffic. By contrast, the Chowan and Roanoke Rivers are among the widest and deepest in all of North Carolina in their lower stretches bordering Bertie. Along their banks thrived a plantation culture based on slave labor and large land holdings. Its residents were part of the wide world of national and international trade, whereas the illiterate and impoverished families of the pocosins inhabited a very different reality in which slavery was uncommon and subsistence farming was the norm.

As reported in the county's 1920 soil survey, "The Roanoke and Chowan Rivers receive directly only a small portion of the drainage waters of the county. Tributaries of the main drainage ways extend to nearly all sections, but the county nevertheless is inadequately drained. . . the more poorly drained areas of the county are included in the Roquist, Buckleberry, and Pell Mell Pocosons and in smaller pocosons. . . the poorly drained portions are the most sparsely settled."

Pell Mell is drier than many of the state's pocosins, some of which support only scattered pines among a predominant growth of shrubs. Bertie is located in the inner coastal plain which is higher in elevation and better drained than the Tidewater areas to the east. Since the 1960s, most pocosins in North Carolina have been drained for conversion to agricultural use, including timber farms as well as fields of cultivated crops. The Pell Mell follows this pattern, although a nucleus of the original "Big Woods" remains intact. The difficulty of paddling upstream to my ancestral lands seems metaphorical for the challenges of genealogical research. The wealthy, literate families along the main waterways left an easily legible historical record. Exploring the world of the Pell Mellers was by contrast an upstream paddle figuratively as well as literally. Their prevalent poverty and illiteracy caused them to leave far fewer historical records than the county's elite. Nevertheless, the documentary record allows us to reconstruct their world in considerable detail.

    Bertie County is the only place on earth where Dunlow and Johnson are equally common names. Most American Dunlows live within a hundred miles of Windsor and have Bertie County roots. Before the Civil War, the name was usually written with three syllables and a wide variety of spellings. After settling in Virginia, [my great-grandfather] Bun and his family dropped the final w for unknown reasons. Whenever I asked about the origin of the name, my Dunlo relatives in Virginia said they had no idea of its source or original spelling, but knew that a middle syllable "de" had been lost in the late nineteenth century, and that all their Carolina cousins spelled the name with a final w. When pressed on the subject they would say that Dundelow sounded Italian. My father conflated the Pell Meller Castellows with Italian Costellos, drawing a parallel suggesting Italian origins for the Dunlows, but Castellaw (the earliest spelling) is actually a Scottish name. In 1977 I took a genealogy class in library school, and learned that my great-great-grandfather was recorded as Josiah Dundelow in Civil War records but as Dunlow usually thereafter. When I first googled the name of Josiah Dunlow back in late 2000, I found two messages from other great-great- grandchildren on a genealogical query site. One had asked about stories he heard from relatives that Josiah was half- or full-blooded Indian, and the other replied that in her family the story was that he was half Indian through his Iroquois mother.

Within a month of beginning my inquiries into my father's family history, I began communicating with David Miller, who was writing a history of the Bertie County Millers and seeking assistance in tracking their descendants. Since my great-grandmother Dunlow was born Lillie Miller, I shared with David what I could find about her descendants. As we exchanged email I learned that David, who had recently retired and was devoting all his energies to genealogy, was quite familiar with local stories of Native ancestry. Some of the Miller lines preserved such tales, and some of the nineteenth-century photographs he collected for his book were of persons who appeared to him to be part Indian. This reminded me that the first I had ever heard about Indian ancestry from Bertie County kinfolk was that Lillie and her brother Uncle Will both had dark hair well into old age as a result of Indian ancestry in the Miller line. After I told him about my interest in the Dunlows and Johnsons, David offered to meet me in Bertie County and show me sites associated with various families of common interest. Starting in the Colerain area where the Millers and Perrys were major landowners, we worked our way down towards Askewville following a meandering path highlighted by historical landmarks, stopping at Ross Baptist Church, where most of our nineteenth- century ancestors had worshipped.

A couple of weeks after my first visit to Askewville with David, I returned alone in search of my Dunlow and Johnson great-great-grandparents' graves. I started by driving down Bull Hill Road towards Windsor from Ross Church. Few houses are located on that stretch of highway, lined with pine forests owned by international corporations, interspersed with a few patches of older mixed woods including that in which the Johnson cemetery was located. Hiking through a pocosin was a new and different experience, unlike either the coastal flatlands of my youth or the Piedmont hills where I now live. The terrain is by no means flat, as the elevation varies about fifty feet. Standing water appears in no particular pattern, just as frequently in the higher elevations as near the Will's Quarter Swamp which flows beside the cemetery. I followed the trail to the cemetery, visible from some distance because of the tall hardwoods.

The graves of Marcus and Rutha Johnson occupied the center of the acre in which Hawkinses and Johnsons were buried in the late nineteenth and early twentieth centuries. After a couple of false starts, I found the right trail out and emerged feeling as if this expedition had been a rite of initiation. Hiking in jungly terrain to the edge of the swamp and a haunted-looking cemetery had probably taken only three miles even including two wrong turns. But in one hour I had reconnected with my lost Johnson family roots symbolically by making this pilgrimage. By the end of the year I had joined three dozen Johnson cousins, all new acquaintances, on a hike to the cemetery through the for- est. It was fortunate that they photographed the area as it was then, because the next time we returned after a reunion in 2003 it was to a bleak, treeless expanse stretching from the road to the swamp. The pine forest was gone.

Despite the stories about Duneleauxs and Calais and French Moselles who became Mizelles, there is no evidence of any of these spellings in local historical records, nor for that matter of any French settlement in Bertie County. On the other hand, there is abundant evidence that Dunlow, Cale, and Mizelle all originated in the British Isles as did virtually all other names of early Bertie settlers. Anna Dunelow, born 1693 in Derbyshire, England, is the earliest family member listed in online records under any spelling; hers is the standard spelling in most subsequent British records.

As I began to investigate my Bertie County roots, I met many cousins distant and not-so-distant, and learned quickly that family traditions about Native American ancestry are very common in the Askewville area, not just among Cales. But there is considerable disagreement about the validity of those traditions.

The earliest mention of a Dunlow by any spelling in Bertie County records was in the May 1774 Court, when Thomas Jones, a seven year old orphan, was apprenticed to Henry Dunnlow to learn the trade of a bricklayer.1 (All spellings are reproduced as written.) This reveals that Dunlows were in Bertie as early as 1774, probably earlier, if the court was willing to grant apprenticeship to Henry, and that Henry was a brickmason rather than a farmer. There is only one additional appearance of the surname in Bertie colonial records. In the August Court of 1775, Henry Dunlow and David and James Curry petitioned the court to be exempted from working on the "new Pell (Peel?) Cypress Road to Windsor." It was ordered that they be exempted from that road, and instead that they work on the new road to the Fork near Wills Quarter Bridge and from the said Wills Quarter. This suggests that Henry lived north of Windsor in the vicinity of the Pell Mell Pocosin, since any land owner or resident who lived along a road was required by law to work on the road nearest him a certain number of days per year.

Henry enlisted in the Continental army as a private on January 26, 1777 and served through January 27, 1780, in Captain Howell Tatum's Company of the First Regiment, commanded by Colonel Thomas Clark.3 In February 1779 Henry was promoted to corporal. Howell Tatum, from Halifax County, was made captain on April 3, 1777 and served three years as company commander before being detached in the spring of 1780 to serve as an aide-de-camp. Tatum was taken prisoner at the Battle of Charleston on May 12, 1780, and not exchanged until June 14, 1781. Completing his service at the beginning of the year, Henry was spared the crushing defeat at Charleston that half destroyed the North Carolina Continental line. At the end of his service Henry was paid eighty pounds, twelve shillings, according to a certificate filed the commissioner of the Hillsborough District. Three years later he was awarded an additional $268 and given a suit of clothes. Henry's surname appears variously as Dunnelloe, Dondalout, and Donally in different military records.

After his military service Henry returned to Bertie County where he remained for most of the 1780s. (Original spellings are preserved in the following paragraphs.) In November 1781, Henry Dunnelo appeared in open court and was discharged on his recognizance. Three months later, in February 1782, a deed from Joseph Collins to Hugh Dunnelo was acknowledged by said Collins and ordered to be registered. Hugh, probably a younger brother since he enlisted three years after Henry, died in 1783, as indicated by an August 1783 court order "that Henry Dunnelo have administration of the estate of Hugh Dunnello dec'd." In November 1783, Henry Dunnelow returned an inventory of Hugh's estate which lists one hundred acres of land, a mare, a two-year-old colt, two cows, a yearling, a feather bed, a saddle, a pewter dish and a plate.

In November 1784 a lawsuit was filed by Henry Dundelow against Joseph Collins and in February 1785 the jury found for the plaintiff. In the same session the court ordered that Henry Dunnelo "Remove his houses off the public lotts." In August 1785 Henry Dunnelow was named in a list of insolvents. He was apparently unable or unwilling to care for his nephew John because six months later the court ordered that "John Dunnelo be bound unto Jesse White to learn the trade of a Cooper." In the same session it was ordered that Elisha Rhodes "take into his possession all the goods and chattels of Hugh Dunnelo decd." in compensation for debts incurred by Henry. In the spring of 1786 a deed of sale of land from the commissioners of Windsor to Henry Dunnelo was proved in open court, indicating that his situation had temporarily improved. But in November 1787 the court ordered that Charney Dundelo "be bound unto Benjamin

Edwards to learn the art and mistery of a Cooper." It would be unusual for him to be apprenticed while his father was alive, since apprentices during this period were generally either orphans or the children of mulattoes, usually of a single female mulatto.

Henry served three years in the Revolution but never received a military land warrant. His only heirs were Lemuel Hosey and wife Sarah of Perquimans County, who on December 6, 1805 authorized Daniel Cherry of Wilson County, Tennessee to act as their attorney. Two days later in Windsor, James Laton and Ezekiel White made a deposition that they had known Sarah Hosea, wife of Lemuel Hosea, since she was an infant, and that she was the only heir of Henry Dondelow who stood mustered for years as a corporal. This was a legislative petition for relief on this issue, suggesting that Henry did not leave written proof of his service. Sarah must have grown up in Bertie County since these witnesses knew her from birth; she is apparently the Sarah Dundelow who married Solomon Sparkman there in 1797. Cherry is a common name in the county, but it is odd that someone who lived in Tennessee would have their power of attorney rather than someone closer to home.

The Secretary of State Revolutionary War papers include a testimony dated May 17, 1820 from Anne Hail. Anne testified that she was legally married to Hugh Donally before he enlisted in the army, and that her son John Donally was Hugh's only heir. Hugh is identified as a private in Captain Dixon's Company. On the same day, John Butler testified under oath that he knew Hugh Donally, was in the company with him at the time of his death, and that he left a son, John Donally, his only heir, then living and a resident of Bertie County. Also on May 20, John Donally gave power of attorney to his lawyer Joseph H. Bryan, "to ask, demand and receive land warrant for the services of his father Hugh Donally, who died in the service." Ten days later it was ordered that a land warrant for 640 acres be issued to the heirs of Hugh Donelly. A considerable number of pension applications claimed service in the Tenth North Carolina Regiment in 1781-82, but this regiment had gone out of existence in 1778. Clerks responsible for pension applications made many such mistaken attributions to the Tenth.

Although Henry Dunlow's origin remains a mystery, his death was recorded in 1793 at Legion Ville, Pennsylvania. He had been living with one female according to a 1787 Bertie census, which could refer to his daughter Sarah or to his wife, but Henry appears in the 1790 census of Halifax County, North Carolina living alone. Later the same year he returned to military service and left North Carolina to serve in the Legion of the United States. When Henry's estate was settled in 1805 Sarah had become the wife of Lemuel Hosey/Hosea in Perquimans.

Patrick Riley, an archaeologist from Pennsylvania, wrote to me in 2002 about the resting place of Henry Dundelow after finding posts I had written about him on the Bertie County genealogical website. His main interest was the preservation of the site of Legion Ville, which is threatened with suburban sprawl in Beaver County near Pittsburgh. Riley had unearthed documents from the camp including a list of those buried in the cemetery. Camp records show that Henry enlisted in North Carolina on September 18, 1790, and died at Legion Ville on January 8, 1793.

The Legion of the United States was established in reaction to an Indian attack on the northwest frontier in what is now northeastern Indiana. Nine tribes had cooperated in an attack on a party led by General Arthur St. Clair, resulting in more than a thousand American deaths. President Washington authorized reorganization of the two existing regiments of the U.S. army and the creation of a third and fourth regiment. A nationwide recruitment campaign ensued, and by the end of

1792, there were 1900 new recruits assembled near Fort Fayette. The new regiments were led by General Anthony Wayne, and two of four sublegions under his command were in the Pittsburgh area.

Although the 1783 peace treaty had required British withdrawal of all armies and garrisons in United States territory, nine years later they still maintained military posts in three places which were within American boundaries specified by the treaty: Detroit, Michilimackinac, and Niagara. Native Americans in the region were divided between pro- and anti-American factions. Preparations of the Legion Ville site began in early November 1792. By the end of that month, soldiers began to arrive at the new encampment on the eastern bank of the Ohio River between two creeks. By Christmas, General Wayne was seriously ill. In early 1793 the place was described as a "first rate winter camp" with huts well-constructed and decorated overlooked by an elegant house for General Wayne. Although contemporary descriptions are of a "happy, healthy, and well-dressed" army, a typhus epidemic had been reported in December 1792, which suggests the probable cause of Henry Dundelow's death.

Henry would have been among the oldest soldiers at Legion Ville if he were the same person who had taken on an apprentice in 1774. He would have been near forty at the time of his death, while most Legion members were no more than thirty-five according to Riley. But the fact that his daughter Sarah was first married in 1797 suggests that Henry was middle aged when he died. Like Henry's daughter Sarah, Hugh Dundelow's son John was granted 640 Tennessee acres for his service, in this case credit for eighty-four months in Captain McRee's Company. This conflicts with the pension correspondence identifying him as a member of Dixon's Company, which must refer to one of two brothers, Henry and Tilghman Dixon, both of whom commanded companies in 1781-82. Griffith John McRee was a captain in the First

Regiment until the Battle of Charleston where he was taken prisoner. In 1781 he was released and continued to serve as an officer until 1798.

John and Charney were both apprenticed around the age of seven. John Dundelow was known to be an orphan, one category of child that was often apprenticed. If Charney was John's brother, his apprenticeship would also have been due to orphan status. But one other category of boy was usually apprenticed: bastards, especially mulattoes. Henry's legal problems began in 1781 with some unspecified minor offense; in 1783 he was administrator of Hugh's estate but by 1785 he was insolvent and the following year Elisha Rhodes, bondsman for his administration of the estate, received all Hugh's goods and chattels (presumably including his land) and John was apprenticed. Henry appears in these documents as incapable of taking care of his nephew, in and out of legal trouble, and impoverished. Sometime between 1787 and 1790, Henry left Bertie County for Halifax. No Dundelows under any spelling are found again in Bertie records until Sarah's marriage to Solomon Sparkman in 1797. Lucy Dundelow appears in marriage records in 1801 marrying David Curry, Jr.

The next appearance of the Dundelow name in Bertie County records is John's marriage to Rhody Cowand in 1803. In 1810, John and Rhody were recorded by the census as living in adjacent Halifax County, but before 1820 they returned to Bertie. Like Henry, they migrated from Bertie to Halifax, the metropolis of the entire Roanoke Valley, but after a few years moved on. Were it not for John and Rhody's decision to return to Bertie, the Dunlows would have merely passed through the county in the late eighteenth century, and never become one of its larger clans in the nineteenth.

Before moving to South Norfolk my great grandparents Bun and Lillie Dunlow sold their twenty acre home place in Askewville to Perry Johnson for $340 on February 15, 1910. The next day Perry and Mary Johnson signed a mortgage deed in the same amount to Alfred Mizell, from whom they had borrowed the money to buy the land. The description in thedeed connects the early twentieth century departure of my ancestors from the Pocosin to their late eighteenth century arrival: "known as the John Butler land and being said William A. Dunlow's home place, containing twenty acres more or less."

This reveals that the land had originally been in the possession of John Butler, Jr. whose daughter Susanah, son John, and granddaughter Eliza all married Dunlows. John Butler, Jr. married Keziah Prichard in 1797; Keziah's brother Jonathan was executor of John Butler, Sr.'s estate, and like him had purchased land from the estate of Cader Bass. Since the Bass family is known to have had Indian ancestry (and still dominates the Nansemond tribe to this day) this suggests a mixed race presence in the Pell Mell as far back as the 1780s. Butlers, Johnsons, Mizelles, and Dunlows continue to live along Askewville Road, but Prichards and Basses are no longer found in the immediate vicinity.

John Butler, Jr. applied for a Revolutionary War pension in November 1820, claiming to be 66 years old. Appearing in open court at the Bertie County Court of Pleas and Quarter Sessions on November 27th, he also claimed that he had been awarded a pension "under the Act of 1818 commencing on the 24th April 1818." Butler reported owning "220 acres of poor barren, piney, marshy, wet, flat land valued by the assessors at 50 cents per acre," and listed his livestock as "3 cows - 3 calves - 1 Heifer - 1 Small horse 14 years old - [and] 22 head of small hogs." He named his family as "his wife Milly, aged 50 years. . . can do but little work...Temperence his daughter aged 18 years who works for herself...Sucky his daughter aged 14 years - able to maintain herself, William his son aged about 16 years able to maintain himself...Abigail his daughter aged 8 years who can do but little towards getting a living." Sucky is a nickname for Susan or Susanah, who married Elmore Dunlow in 1830.

Her father claimed to have enlisted in Windsor for a term of two and a half years, and to have served in "Captain Jeremiah McLayen or McLean's company in the Regiment commanded by Col. Thomas Polk in the North Carolina line" adding that he "fought in the Battle of Charleston, S.C. and was discharged at Halifax, N.C. at the expiration of his term." This was the same company in which Ezekiel White served during the same years. John Butler's marriage to Keziah Prichard was recorded on 27 December 1797 with her brother Christopher Prichard as bondsman.

The account of the May 1815 estate sale reveals that Butler's son-in-law Jonathan Prichard, estate administrator, bought fourteen items, twice as many as the next most frequent buyer, granddaughter Susanah. Prichard purchased a frying pan, an iron wedge, a horse collar, a reap hook and chest, five knives, a sleigh, a brandy barrel, four other barrels, a keg, a box, five stocks of bees, and five books. Susanah bought one rawhide, a pot, five chairs, a tray meal tub and sifter, a loom and gear, a box, a fat tub, and two pigs. Neither of her parents, nor any of her siblings, were listed as participating in the sale, so it is possible that she was acting on behalf of her entire family.

John Butler Sr.'s 1807 will named his wife Winifred and children John, Silas Butler, Sarah, Dycey, and Martha. Since the widow is not mentioned in the estate sale dated eight years after the will, apparently John Butler Sr. died before 1810 and the estate sale occurred after the death of the widow; two Winifred Butlers appear as heads of household in the 1810 Bertie census. Martha Butler was the wife of Jonathan Prichard. The absence of the male Butler children in the estate papers has a possible military explanation. Silas and John P. Butler both sENDNOe rved in McDonald's Company of the First North

Carolina Militia in 1814 and 1815, as did their kinsman Curry Butler. The estate sale for John Butler, Jr. took place on October 10, 1828, with nephew Jarvis Butler as administrator. Total sales amounted to $152.93. The widow was the most frequent buyer, purchasing fourteen items. Everet and Jarvis Butler purchased twelve and seven items respectively. Susanah was the only other participant buying more than three items: a lot of plows, a lot of earthen ware, a flat iron, and a feather bed. Although still unmarried, she appeared to be anticipating setting up housekeeping. Her future father-in-law, John Dunelow, bought one barrow hog, and Jethro Butler bought one black yearling.

On October 13, 1786, John Butler, Sr. bought twenty acres "called Keough field" neighboring Cader Bass from John and Esther White, the sale witnessed by Cader Bass and Ezekiel White. On May 1, 1792, Butler bought 150 acres and buildings thereon from George West, executor of the estate of Cader Bass, "on the east side of Pell Mell Pocoson" adjacent to his own land and neighboring Jonathan Miller, Aaron Asbell, and James Sowell. On the same day Butler bought another fifty acres from the same estate. These are clearly purchases by These are clearly purchases by John Sr., since he appears in a 1798 tax list owning 170 acres wherein his son John does not appear at all. The name John Butler next appears in a deed dated January 25, 1806, buying twelve acres "in the fork of Long branch" neighboring George Outlaw for fifty-two silver dollars.

More than 80 per cent of heads of families counted as 'all other free persons' in the 1790-1810 federal census for North Carolina were descendants of free African Americans from colonial Virginia. These families were well accepted by their white neighbors, and petitions for repeal of a discriminatory tax were signed by leading white citizens in several counties during the late colonial period. In Bertie and several neighboring counties, free African Americans constituted about five per cent of the free population and most were landowners.

The history of the land owned by John Butler reveals that the Pell Mell Pocosin was distinctive not only for the mulatto status of many of its early settlers, but also for their relative prosperity and acceptance by white society.

Cader Bass, from whom the Butler land was purchased, belonged to a family that was regarded as of mixed race, Nansemond Indian and English. In an effort to maintain title to tribal lands William Bass of Norfolk County, Virginia, obtained a certificate from the County Court Clerk in 1727 which certified "no admixture of negor, Ethiopic blood."41 His wife was Sarah Lovina, the daughter of John Nichols and his "negro woman" Judith Lovina.

In a will dated April 12, 1775 and proved in the August Court of that year, Henry Bunch named as his grandson Cader Bass, son of his daughter Nancy and Isaac Bass. The Bunch and Bass families were two of the largest landowners among the free mulattoes of northeastern North Carolina, and some were slaveholders as well. Although Isaac had been taxed in Bertie County in 1756, and his wife's family was likewise classified as mulatto, he relocated to what is now Edgecombe County, where after his death his children were classified as white. He left nine slaves in his will, proved February 1801. Isaac outlived his son Cader by nine years. Cader remained in Bertie when the rest of the family moved west, and was the major beneficiary when his grandfather Henry Bunch died in 1775. Owning one slave and 450 acres in 1779, Cader was among the handful of mulatto slaveholders in Bertie County. Although no legitimate offspring are documented, in August 1787 he posted bond for a bastard child borne by Sarah Farmer, daughter of Joseph Farmer, a "free Mulatto" head of household in John Hill's 1763 list.

Henry Bunch Sr. resided in Chowan County when he first purchased 200 acres of land in Bertie County in 1727. Thisoriginal farm was located on Reedy Branch, but two years later he added another 640 acres on Connaritsa Swamp to his holdings, purchased from Thomas Pollock. In tax lists for 1750 and 1763 he was a free mulatto taxable owning two slaves. When he died in 1775 he had already deeded 840 acres of land on Connaritsa and Mulberry swamps to his grandson Jeremiah Bunch, Jr. Most of the land on which he lived at the time of his death was willed to Cader Bass.

APPENDIX: SOUTH NORFOLK FAMILY PHOTOGRAPHS

Willie Dunlo, Mamie Johnson front, Susan Lillie Miller and James Gray Dunlo back row

Ray, Freddy Johnson

John Henry Johnson

Arthur Eugene Rice, 1879-1936, Eva Belle Haskett, 1886-1959, wedding September 1906

Freddy and Betty Johnson as newlyweds, 1942

ENDNOTES

1 Floyd Moore, *Friends in the Carolinas*. (Greensboro: North Carolina Yearly Meeting of Friends, 1971), 8.

2 Seth Hinshaw, *The Carolina Quaker Experience*, (Greensboro: North Carolina Yearly Meeting of Friends, North Carolina Friends Historical Society, 1984), 6-8.

3 Ibid, 8.

4 Ibid, 15.

5 George Bishop, *New England Judged by the Spirit of the Lord* (London,T. Sowle, 1703), 258-259.

6 Paul D. Escott, *Many Excellent People: Power and Privilege in NorthCarolina, 1750-1900* (Chapel Hill: UNC Press, 1988), 72.

7 Hiram Hilty, *Toward Freedom for All: North Carolina Quakers andSlavery*. (Richmond, Ind: Friends United Press, 1984), 31.

8 Stephen B. Weeks, *Southern Quakers and Slavery: A Study in Institutional History* (Baltimore: Johns Hopkins Press, 1896), 261.

9 Hilty, *Toward Freedom for All*, 40.

10 Ibid, 43.

11 Email from Gwen Gosney Erickson, Archivist, Friends HistoricalCollection, Guilford College.

12 Claude Andrew Clegg, *The Price of Liberty: African Americans and theMaking of Liberia* (Chapel Hill: UNC Press, 2004), 55.

13 Ibid.

14 Eric Foner, ed., *Nat Turner* (Englewood Cliffs, NJ: Prentice-Hall), 61.

15 Jean Fagan Yellin, *Harriet Jacobs: A Life* (New York: Basic Civitas Books, 2004), 38.

16 Harriet Jacobs, *Incidents in the Life of a Slave Girl* (Mineola, N.Y.:Dover, 2001), 55-56.

17 Ibid, 58.

18 Ibid.

19 William Twine White service record.

20 Email from Miles Sandin.

21 Frances Harding Casstevens, *Edward A. Wild and the African Brigadein the Civil War* (Jefferson, NC: MCFarland, 2003), p. 53.

22 Ibid, 63.

23 Ibid, 67.

24 Ibid, 69.

25 Ibid, 77.

26 Ibid, 93.

27 Ibid, 94.

28 Ibid, 103.

29 *War of the Rebellion: a Compilation of the Official Records of the Unio nand Confederate Armies* (Washington: Government Printing Office, 1899), Series II,

Volume VI, 1129-1130..
30 Casstevens, Edward Wild, p. 107.
31 Ibid, 111.
32 Ibid, 123.
33 Ibid.
34 Ibid, 124.
35 Ibid, 142.
36 Ibid, 191.

Chapter 1

1 Collins, "Eastern North Carolinians in the Union Army," 1.
2 Ibid., 2.
3 Ibid., 4.
4 Josiah Dunlow military records.
5 Thomas, Bertie in Blue, 86.
6 Collins, "Eastern North Carolinians in the Union Army," 6.
7 Ibid., 7.
8 Thomas, Bertie in Blue, vii.
9 Ibid., viii.
10 Trotter, Ironclads and Columbiads, 1.
11 Ibid., 211.
12 Thomas, Bertie in Blue, 7.
13 Idem.
14 Idem.
15 Ibid., 9.
16 Ibid., 11.
17 Ibid., 13.
18 Official Records, Vol. I, 45-49.
19 Thomas, Bertie in Blue, 15-16.
20 Rigdon, 32nd Infantry, 110; Thomas, Divided Allegiances, 101.
21 Thomas, Bertie in Blue, 36.
22 Idem.
23 Ibid., 17.
24 Ibid., 18.
25 Ibid., 19.
26 Ibid., 21-23.
28 Idem.
29 Ibid., 32
30 Ibid., 33.
31 Idem.
32 Thomas, Bertie in Blue, 35.

33 Ibid., 64.
34 Butler, Pirates, Privateers, and Rebel Raiders of the Carolina Coast, 138.
35 Branch, Fort Macon as a Shelter for Buffaloes, 1.
36 Ibid., 2.
37 Idem.
38 Idem.
39 Ibid., 3.
40 Idem.
41 Thomas, *Bertie in Blue*, 39.

Chapter Two

1 Speer, *Portals to Hell*, 259.
2 Ibid., 261.
3 Ibid., 264.
4 Ibid., 265.
5 Ibid, xiv.
6 Marcus Johnson military records.
7 Bishir, The Historic Architecture of Eastern North Carolina,
8 Weitz, More Damning than Slaughter, xix.
9 North Carolina Troops 1861-1865, 69.
10 Weitz, More Damning than Slaughter, 10.
11 Ibid., 12-13.
12 Ibid., 13.
13 Ibid., 191.
14 Ibid., 192.
15 Idem.

Chapter Three

1 Freehling, *The South vs. the South*, xiii.
2 Ibid., 202.
3 Neel, The Wilford-Williford Treks into America, 19.
4 Idem.
5 Mary Williford estate papers, 1841.
8 Ludie Hughes bastardy bond, 1844.
9 Wiley Askew deeds.
10 Bertie County Rootsweb site.
11 John Hughes apprentice paper.
12 Thomas, Divided Loyalties, 46.

13North Carolina Troops 1861-1865, 69
14Wiley Askew 1891 estate papers.
15"Cyclone in North Carolina," Atlanta Constitution, May 24, 1892.

Chapter Four

1Escott, *Many Excellent People*, 4
2Ibid., 7
3Ibid., 63
4 "It Becomes My Duty to Inform You," *Poor Town Gazette* No. 62 (online journal.)
5Cecil-Fronsmann, *Common Whites*, 7
6Ibid., 13.
7Browning, "Little Souled Mercenaries?", 339.
8Anderson, *Race and Politics in North Carolina, 1872-1901*, 34
9Ibid., 79
10Ibid., 199
12*Windsor Ledger*, January 6, 1898.
13Ibid, May 12, 1898.
14Ibid., November 10, 1898.
15Winston, *It's a Far Cry,* 52
16Anderson, *Race and Politics*, 256
17Ibid., 335

SOURCES CITED

Alther, Lisa, *Kinfolks: Falling off the Family Tree, the Search for My Melungeon Ancestors.* New York: Arcade, 2007.

Anderson, Eric, *Race and Politics in North Carolina, 1872-1901: The Black Second.* Baton Rouge: LSU Press, 1981.

Barrett, John, *North Carolina as a Civil War Battleground 1861-1865.* Raleigh: Division of Archives and History, 1984.

Bishir, Catherine, *A Guide to the Historic Architecture of Eastern North Carolina.* Chapel Hill: University of North Carolina Press, 1996.

Branch, Paul, "Fort Macon as a Shelter for Buffaloes," *Ramparts,* Spring 1997.

Browning, Judkin Jay, "'Little Souled Mercenaries'? The Buffaloes of Eastern North Carolina during the Civil War." *The North Carolina Historical Review,* LXXVII: 3 (July 2000), pp. 337-363.

Cecil-Fronsman, Bill, *Common Whites: Class and Culture in Antebellum North Carolina.* Lexington:University Press of Kentucky, 1992.

Collins, Joseph E., "Eastern North Carolinians in the Union Army: The First and Second North Carolina Union Volunteer Regiments." Online edition http://homepages.rootsweb.com/~ncuv/collins1.htm

"Cyclone in North Carolina," The Atlanta Constitution, May 24, 1892. Reprinted in http://www.rootsweb.com/~usgenweb/ncetie.htm

Dunstan, Edythe Smith, The Bertie Index for Court-house Records of Bertie Co., (1720-1875). N.p., 1966.

Escott, Paul D., *Many Excellent People: Power and Privilege in North Carolina, 1850-1900.* Chapel Hill: University of North Carolina Press, 1985.

Freehling, William, *The South vs. the South.* Oxford and New York: Oxford University Press, 2001.

Haun, Wynette Parks, *Bertie County North Carolina Court Minutes.* Durham, W.P. Haun, 1976-1984.

Hilty, Hiram H., *Toward Freedom for All*: North Carolina Quakers and Slavery. Richmond, IN: Friends United Press, 1982.

Manarin, Louis H., ed., *North Carolina Troops, 1861-1865: a Roster.* Raleigh: State Department of Archives and History, 1966.

Neel, Eurie Pearl Wilford, *The Wilford-Williford Treks Into America.* N.p., 1959.

Pearce, James B., "It Becomes My Duty to In- form You," Poor Town Gazette No. 62, http://pages.prodigy.net/jabeckpearce/poor_town/front/62frontpage.htm.

Smallwood, Arvin, *Bertie County: An Eastern Carolina History.* Charleston: Arcadia, 2002.

Speer, Lonnie, *Portals to Hell.* Mechanicsburg, PA: Stackpole Books, 1997.

Thomas, Gerald, *Bertie in Blue.* Plymouth, N.C.: Jones Printing, 1997.

Thomas, Gerald, *Divided Loyalties.* Raleigh: Division of Archives and History, 1996.

Thompson, Harry, *Bertie Folklore.* Plymouth, N.C., Jones Printing, 2002.

Trotter, William, *Ironclads and Columbiads: the Coast.* Winston-Salem: John S. Blair, 1991.

U. S. Navy Department, The War of the Rebellion: A Compilation of the Official Records of the Union and Confederate Navies (Washington: Government Printing Office, 1880-1927)

Weitz, Mark A., *More Damning Than Slaughter: Desertion in the Confederate Army.* Lincoln: University of Nebraska Press, 2005.

Winston, Robert, *It's a Far Cry.* New York: Holt, 1937.

Made in the USA
Middletown, DE
05 October 2024